The Russian People Speak

The Russian People Speak

Democracy at the Crossroads

Nikolai Popov

SYRACUSE UNIVERSITY PRESS

First Edition 1995
95 96 97 98 99 00 6 5 4 3 2 1

The paper used in this publication meets the minimum requirements of American National Standard for Information Sciences—Permanence of Paper for Printed Library Materials, ANSI Z39.48-1984. ∞™

Library of Congress Cataloging-in-Publication Data

Popov, N. P. (Nikolaĭ Petrovich)
The Russian people speak : democracy at the crossroads / Nikolai Popov.
p. cm.
Includes bibliographical references (p.).
ISBN 0-8156-0300-2.
1. Russia (Federation)—Social conditions—1991- —Public opinion. 2. Post-communism—Russia (Federation)—Public opinion. 3. Public opinion—Russia (Federation). I. Title.
HN530.2.Z9P876 1994
306′.0947—dc20 94-36314

Manufactured in the United States of America

To the three girls in my life:
Katya, Dasha, Nastya

Nikolai P. Popov, Head of the Political Surveys Department, Russian Center for Public Opinion Research, Moscow, was senior analyst of Western public opinion trends at the USSR's Institute of U.S.-Canada Studies and has been a frequent contributor to the publications *Sovetskaya Cultura* and *Moscow News*.

Contents

Tables

Preface

What has happened in the last ten years to the former Soviet Union is an event of enormous historical significance. In the twentieth century it can only be compared to the rise of two aggressive totalitarian systems, German fascism and the communist empire in Russia. The destruction of one totalitarian system and more recently the breakdown of the other offer hope that an era of uninterrupted cooperation and development within the world community is about to begin.

These horrible upheavals of the twentieth century have taught people, through tragic experience, that the uncontrollable power of the state, despite its benevolent slogans, inevitably leads to the suppression of individual and collective freedoms, to the subordination of personality, and to the intimidation, suffering, and even genocide of unprotected groups. This unrestricted power of the state has endangered the very existence of life on this planet.

The lesson we have learned would be incomplete if we do not try to understand fully how these diabolical systems developed and what caused their dissolution. It is very important for the future of our world to apprehend why the Soviet system existed for so long and why it collapsed so abruptly. And an additional question should also be raised: is the Soviet system's dissolution final or is there a chance of putting the system together again, with a corresponding menace to world stability and the newly acquired freedom of its subjects?

To answer these questions, it is important to ascertain how powerful the Soviet totalitarian system was and what held it together beyond its system of fear and military might. Was there mass support for the system or did it lack this support? Was the Soviet system a "colossus on clay feet," as Hitler believed, or was the giant supported by—besides the repressive military and bureaucratic machine—a special political culture that "overcame the masses"? And if such a political culture or "Soviet civilization" did exist and supported the system, to what extent was it destroyed by the radical changes and reforms of recent years—or was it destroyed at all?

In other words, to what extent are the Russian people, as well as other peoples of Russia and the former Soviet Union, ready to accept, support, and partake in democratic reforms, or are these reforms doomed to failure and is restoration of the old rules inevitable, in one form or another?

This monograph attempts to answer some of these questions, using both traditional sources including mass media accounts and rare printed sources, and most importantly the results of public opinion polling, until recently nonexistent as a research tool in a communist country. With the beginning of democratization and glasnost, public opinion polling has begun and is now playing an important role in the democratic process of feedback—from the masses to the rulers.

The author has used the results of his own surveys, as well as other polls conducted by the Russian Center for Public Opinion and Market Research (VCIOM), the only nationwide organization conducting mass polling to date. Other scarce polling data were also used.

The author has also employed his own personal experiences within the totalitarian system to comprehend and explain how the system was supported and why it collapsed so suddenly. These experiences include participation in most of its political institutions for five out of seven decades of the system's history—with the lucky exception of gulag—Young Pioneer organization, secondary schools, Komsomol, the university, party and labor union organizations, the press, the diplomatic corps, and academic institutions. The present author has sampled all forms of political and cultural indoctrination aimed at the creation of the "new Soviet man," which is the very basis of the system to be discussed.

Moscow, Russia
January 1994

Nikolai Popov

The Russian People Speak

1

Introduction

What we are witnessing in Russia, and in the former Soviet Union, is the disintegration not only of the USSR but also of an empire of unprecedented scale, the "Eastern Bloc" or "socialist camp." We are also observing the breakup of a totalitarian system, which dominated this area of the globe and which was spreading its influence to other continents as well.

Because the empire had developed geographically and sociopolitically into a huge, interconnected system, it could not sustain this size and began breaking up as a system, like a skyscraper during an earthquake—at all its joints and levels. As the ailing Soviet giant lost its footing, the "socialist camp" almost simultaneously began to free itself from communist dictatorship and from Soviet domination. Within a few months, the Soviet Union broke into many separate states, and the waves of separatism began crashing on Russia's shores.

Democracy in Russia had begun its slow and painful ascent. Since February 1990 the country has ceased to operate under a system of one-party rule, and the Communist party is no longer the ruling party. It no longer dictates, as it had for seven decades, all political, economic, and cultural processes and organizations.

What we see now is a period of political vacuum, an interregnum. The dictatorship of the Communist party may have come to an end, but it has not been replaced by any real political alternative. The country's newly created parties are weak and lack a political foundation.

The Soviet planned economy was on the verge of a crisis at the beginning of perestroika. The end of totalitarian control, which resulted in the dissolution of economic ties among the former Soviet republics, has moved the country closer to a state of chaos, with sky-rocketing inflation, decreased industrial and agricultural production, and an impoverished populace.

Transition from one system to another, even from a nonmetric to a metric system, is always difficult. The transition from a planned economy in a totalitarian system to one that is market-driven and self-governing is inevitably a painful and dramatic leap, no matter how smooth the economists and government leaders might suggest it to be.

One important phenomenon from this period of transition has been the dramatic increase in ethnic problems, which often resulted in open conflicts and bloody clashes. These conflicts were not always rooted in national tensions or old antagonisms, but they were manifested in people of different nationalities fighting each other.

These dramatic changes are accompanied by further deterioration in public morality and social standards, by increases in violence and crime, and by an escalation in the antagonisms that arise among different social classes and groups.

Why do so many problems exist at once? Why is the social fabric of the country falling apart in so many places simultaneously? Why does all this chaos and unpredictability exist?

The Soviet Union has been in the grip of totalitarian rule much longer than other countries in Eastern Europe. The deterioration of this society is deep and all-encompassing and, consequently, even the traces of civic society have been eradicated.

Also missing are the traditions associated with democratic institutions and with the family farm: the development of entrepreneurial skills, the nurturing of initiative, and the encouragement of diversity and independence in art and culture.

The chief damage caused by seven decades of totalitarian rule under the Communist party is not seen in the economy, although the country's standing among industrial nations and their standards of living is at the bottom. The main damage can be seen in its effect on the people of the Soviet Union and Russia.

The Soviet people, and the Russian people in particular, have sustained enormous losses in human life. More than 40 million people were exterminated by the repressive Communist regime itself. More than 27 million were lost in a war, which the totalitarian regime had helped to start, and for which it was ill-prepared to fight. These staggering losses among the most active members of the populace could not help but result in genetic damage to the Soviet people, damage that has yet to be assessed.

But no less tragic are the consequences of these seven decades on the mass public consciousness, consequences documented in sociological studies that are being manifested in the process of disintegration now threatening the country.

Seven decades of living with these horrible human losses and living under conditions of constant fear have molded a special form of human being distinguished by specific, if not unique, characteristics and known generally as *Homo soveticus.*

What are those characteristics?

One of the most salient aspects of Soviet mass consciousness is the absence of public opinion. Decades of fear—with a simultaneous growth in political apathy and conformity—have resulted in a mass consciousness characterized by an undeveloped political culture. In order to survive, generations of Soviet citizens have learned not to have an opinion on the important issues of the day.

Therefore, what Russians are measuring today through public opinion polling is the painful, erratic process of "birth," and most importantly, the birth of individual opinion, individual reckoning, and personal judgment.

Many of our mass views have been formed only recently; they are superficial in nature and could better be described as emotions, moods, or vague impressions. More often than not they are negations of existing practices, rather than constructive views on ways to solve problems or rebuild society.

The absence of a political culture, of real choice, of plurality in the marketplace of ideas, of the tradition to have a personal opinion—this vacuum has resulted in the somewhat paradoxical mixture or blend of modern public views.

These views often include newly formed and, frequently, liberal attitudes on the concrete issues of everyday life alongside more conservative views on theoretical issues, which are throwbacks to the era of forced indoctrination. Practical liberalism and theoretical conservatism are now joint features of individual and group consciousness.

The undeveloped and superficial nature of these views has resulted in an extremely volatile mass consciousness. Public opinion in Russia can alter support for a policy today into a complete rejection of the same policy tomorrow, from a love affair with a politician on any given day to a contempt and repudiation of that politician a few months later. The volatility and instability of public opinion will plague reformers and politicians for a long time to come.

The eradication of Christian morality and any system of humanitarian values in favor of Communist principles has lead to an erosion of public morality, mixed with widespread anomie and moral-ethical negativism. People are alienated from one another, from their institutions, and from the society at large. Whatever held people together in society—the brotherhood of socialism, though hypocritical and propagandistic—has now given way to open egoism, fierce competition, and hostility. As a result, political, economic, and nationalistic conflicts have become more fierce, and violence and crime are in an upsurge.

This moral negativism is accompanied by an ideological vacuum, an inability to visualize or articulate such concepts like the ideal structure for a society, the nation's future goals, the meaning of human existence, or the purpose of humanitarian values. There is little of what is called *weltanschauung*.

Although Communist ideals, for the most part, are viewed critically or skeptically, there has been no movement toward an alternative ideology. Most people have repudiated Marx, but they have not yet embraced humanism, Christianity, or any other ideology.

Soviet mass consciousness is characterized by heterogeneity, fragmentation, and separateness. The artificial proclamations and propagandistic pictures of the "moral-political unity of the Soviet people" and "friendship of people of the USSR" have given way to an intense period of polarization along national, economic, political, religious, age, and other lines.

This fragmentation, this lack of a coherent, unifying system of views and attitudes that are shared by most of the population, will be the foundation of future conflicts, including potentially a civil war.

These qualities of the Soviet mass consciousness will guide the formation of public attitudes for a long time to come. They will shape public life, the process of social change, and the political behavior of individuals and groups.

Even though the Russian political culture is still in its formative stage and mass consciousness remains volatile and contradictory, public opinion polling is the only reliable instrument of feedback from the people to political institutions, including government. Public opinion polls have already become part of political life; they are widely used and misused. Opposing political groups are quoting different poll results, picking those polls that best suit their purposes. As with many other aspects of the emerging political culture in Russia, the polling science and business are still far from perfect. Following the needs of a political market, many nonprofessional polling organizations (including "experts" hired by politicians lacking any sense of responsibility) and the media's own polling groups produce surrogate "straw polls," a trend that belatedly repeats the polling history of other countries.

This book's aim is to determine public attitudes about the departing communist regime, to represent the public's acceptance of the new concepts of democracy and market economy, and to assess the public's involvement in current radical changes in Russia, all by using scarce public opinion polling data. Obviously, there were no sociological surveys or objective analyses of public opinion throughout Stalin's regime. The beliefs of people in the 1960s and the 1970s were examined from different perspectives by Vladimir Shlappentoch[1] and Alexander Zinoviev,[2] while the later years of reform were analyzed in the works of Tatiana Zaslavskaya,[3] Rosalina Ryvkina,[4] Boris Grushin,[5] and Yuri Levada.[6]

But the main sources of information about the views and feelings of people of the Soviet era are the literary works—the fiction and the documentaries. And the most tragic and clear descriptions belong to the authors of the literature of the gulag, such as Alexander Solzhenitsyn, Varlam Shalamov, Oleg Volkov, and Yuri Razgon. Their precise yet emotional descriptions of people who have gone through the Leninist-Stalinist inferno help reconstruct the unreal "other" life of "victorious socialism" and the reality of slavery in the twentieth century.

The pictures of "life on the surface," of those not victimized but rewarded by the system, are made more real, thanks to glasnost, through the publication of novels by Anatoly Rybakov, Vassily Grossman, Fasil Iskander, and Anatoly Pristavkin.

The mass media publications, especially from the post-Stalinist period, provide some glimpses of real life, allowing people's feelings sometime to show through the sugarcoating of official propaganda.

Because the sociological data are available only for the last few years, the sections of this book based on the opinion surveys are supplemented with an analysis of the social processes of the last decades and with attempts to reconstruct from literature and personal experience the views, beliefs, and values of people from the Russian totalitarian past.

In chapter 2 an effort is made to describe the beginning of reforms during that period called perestroika, which has come to be associated with the name of Mikhail Gorbachev. How did it begin? Was the breakdown of the system inevitable or simply accidental? What were the alternatives to reform, and why did the "perfection of socialism" not work? Public reaction to the accelerating reforms and other dramatic changes is also examined.

Chapter 3 addresses the failure of the attempts to create a "new man" during the socialist era and the types of people and personalities which in fact were created by the political culture of socialism.

The public's political views in the former Soviet Union and Russia are discussed in chapter 4. The political culture during the transition period from socialism to democracy is analyzed, along with the public's views concerning political instability and volatility.

Chapter 5 deals with public movement from the socialist ideals of a caring and concerned state to the temptations connected with entrepreneurial activities. Also considered are attitudes toward economic reform and the transition to a market economy.

Chapter 6 is devoted to the breakdown of the totalitarian value system of socialism, and to the growing moral vacuum and anomie that followed it.

Finally, chapter 7, while summarizing the contents of the previous chapters, is also a difficult attempt to forecast the development of events unfolding in Russia in the near future, especially the public mood.

The goals of this book do not allow me to arrange the narration in chronological order; rather, I have described these same historical periods through analyses of the different aspects of society—the political, the economic, and the moral.

2

Perestroika

Socialism with an Honest Face

Reforms in Russia, even if they do not impress its citizens with their successes, are astonishing to many people abroad for their unpredictable drama. Gorbachev begins the restructuring, perestroika, controlled by the party, but then the party loses its limitless power. The communist bloc and then the Soviet Union itself fall apart; a putsch almost frustrates the early stages of democratization. Gorbachev is forced to resign. Yeltsin bans the Communist party and starts radical economic reforms. The resistance of the old power structures to return the country to its totalitarian past, do not end; a second putsch shakes the country.

The people are used to these dreadful upheavals: price increases and the fear of future chaos have somewhat overshadowed in the public's eye the important events, which began in mid-1980s and which ended climactically at the end of 1991. The public half-understands that a tremendously important stage of Russian and Soviet history has concluded, followed by an equally important, yet chronologically insignificant period of six years—from the beginning of perestroika until Gorbachev's departure.

People are not likely to flinch when hearing that the perestroika of socialism has ended and that the formation of a capitalist society has begun. Communist ideas have ceased to be sacrosanct. For some they have become an object for mockery, for others a source of nostalgia. One by one, party chiefs from the past are being thrown off their pedestals; their actions are being excoriated on city squares and in the mass media. Even Lenin is being depicted more and more as a vicious genius and a cruel dictator, and neither the general public nor the political followers of communism objects. Only suggestions to close down the Mausoleum and the Lenin Museum cause bursts of indignation as the last symbols of a departing epoch are being challenged.

One can understand the political weariness and indifference of the public, but to understand what the process has been and why it all began (we'll call it *perestroika,* for convenience) is very important for all of us on both sides of the Atlantic. Were all these truly revolutionary reforms inevitable and determined by history, or was it just another reckless experiment perpetrated on our long-suffering land by a group of adventurers seeking power, glory, and a place in the history books? If the process had been inevitable, if the Gulf Stream of history had picked up and begun to move our social ship, and Gorbachev, not afraid to get on the bridge, turned out to be the right captain at the right moment, we would then have nothing to do but to continue the course and patiently endure our current misfortunes. Even if turning back were the wish of many people, it is now as impossible and as meaningless as an attempt to swim against the stream.

But if perestroika were a mistake—an experiment without a clear goal or proper plan, another collectivization or Khruschev corn-growing campaign, another unsuccessful attempt to catch up with the West (this time, with civilization and democracy)—it is hard to persuade the people of the necessity for further impoverishment and for the dissolution of the Union. It is especially hard to convince them because more than half of the public, according to the polls, wants to return everything to the way it was before 1985. It is difficult to expect successful reforms if society is overcome by inertia through nostalgic feelings for a past life. What makes these people angry is not simply what is being done to them now. They don't understand the purpose behind all the hardship. What were the reasons for starting all this? Where are we going and what are we building (for we were always building something)? The public doesn't know whether they will ever have a normal existence—or, at least, the "normal" existence they had before. If nobody tries to persuade the people that these reforms are inevitable and that the hardships are not endless, political demagogues are sure to appear who will promise a return to "normal" life before perestroika, ruling with an iron fist, reintroducing discipline and order, and eliminating speculators, the underground economy, the new bourgeoisie, etc.

So why did it all start?

Was There a Way Out?

There is a rather widespread explanation about the causes of perestroika. This version concludes that Soviet society was beginning to understand the necessity for change and was beginning to feel dissatisfaction with iron party control, the rigid, ineffective economic system, the low living standards, and the general stagnation. In other words, society was determined to put an end to stagnation and to start reforms.

But what in fact occurred was nothing of the sort. At the beginning of the 1980s, the system was rather stable and balanced. People were still cut off from the rest of the world by the iron curtain and could compare their existence only with the one they had had previously, which was similar or even worse. Propaganda worked strenuously to persuade people of the advantages of socialism and the drawbacks of capitalism. Most of the public accepted this propaganda, and even if they had doubts about it, they could not check it and simply kept silent. The intelligentsia and the politically sophisticated became accustomed to the lie, and they unloaded their feelings using anecdotes told in the kitchen. Some criticism of the system's "isolated" and "rare" defects was allowed. This dose of allowed criticism was carefully measured by the party apparatus, and dissent was suppressed by the all-seeing KGB. Gulag camps were still in existence and not empty. "Our tanks" were still "quick," as the song goes, ready to move in the event of a new Hungary or Czechoslovakia or for internal "riots," as in Novocherkassk.

Throughout the period of communist totalitarian rule, several generations were reared with a purely Soviet mentality, not knowing or imagining any other life. Over the past two decades, penetrability of the iron curtain has led to a somewhat softened ideological core of beliefs and to negotiating a compromise formula—life is richer there, but here it is more reliable. This weakened devotion to ideology was not accompanied or replaced by an alternative ideology or by any inspiration to revise the existing order with radical reforms; it expressed itself only in doleful dissatisfaction with life and in a continuing, but rather sluggish, support of the system and its "principles" and "achievements." Although various problems were identified, several beliefs that were important to the system took root in the mass consciousness. They include: (1) a silent acknowledgement of the ruling elite's absolute power and of the inevitability or even necessity of the "rulers'" total control over all aspects of life; (2) a feeling in an individual of dependency on the state and confidence that the state will solve all economic and social problems; (3) the belief in the equal distribution of wages or salaries; (4) the valuing of equality and social justice over freedom; and (5) a feeling of blending with the masses and hostility toward individuality, personal success, and initiative.

Besides this general public support, the system fed many layers of people: the party apparatus; the millions of bureaucrats of all levels; the komsomol and trade union elite; the creative strata—writers, artists, journalists, and movie men "devoted to the party and the people" and rewarded with trips abroad and other small doses of freedom. Certainly this elite mixed its devotion with cynicism, but the "carrot and the stick" worked reliably and provided support for the system.

Only the youth, growing up in the Brezhnev years, could be dangerous. The system's hypocrisy was patent with, on the one hand, the propaganda of "bright ideals" and the "moral code of a young builder of communism" and, on the other, the obvious and universal corruption, the personal enrichment of the ruling elite and komsomol bureaucracy. This hypocrisy led a sizable part of the youth toward cynicism and selfishness and toward an envy of the Western lifestyle. This stratum of discontent was constantly growing, but it would only become dangerous for the system later on, when the "good-for-nothing" youth of the 1970s acquired real social weight. Still there was an opportunity for the system to absorb these rebels, just as it had neutralized and absorbed most of the liberals of the 1960s.

In a word, the system was stable. Its decay, stagnation, and growing absurdity could have lasted for many more years. There were no signs of self-disintegration.

There was, however, one problem. To keep the system stable, a constant external threat was needed. This threat was required to justify their isolation from the rest of the world and to maintain the arms race, and, within the "beleagured fortress" atmosphere, to keep "moral and political unity," suppress criticism and dissent, and strengthen the dictatorship through the party and the KGB. Moreover, to sustain the ideology, the system needed to support and extend world socialism as far as possible. In other words, the system needed to continue the confrontation with the West under various new names—detente, peaceful coexistence, and competition.

The Soviet Union began to lose this competition with the West despite the efforts of the military-industrial complex to squeeze all the life out of the country. The period of military balance, achieved in the 1960s, was coming to an end; the technical lag was growing, and the economy could hardly support the burden placed on it by the military.

It was becoming clear to many in the higher echelons that the country could not continuously increase its production of modern arms, with their expensive electronics, and maintain a huge and modern army. It was necessary either to reduce military arrogance and the international ambitions of a superpower or to modernize the socialist economic system and allow for some political relaxation. That dilemma had first arisen in the early 1970s. Brezhnev's detente was an effort, without any real changes domestically, to negotiate with the U.S. a reduction in the level of military confrontation and an agreement for reliable game rules. All this had come at a time when the world socialist system continued to expand, into Angola, Nicaragua, El Salvador, and in the Middle East, and the boundaries for the spheres of influence were being redrawn with the West. This effort eventually failed and by the 1980s the problem of reform arose anew.

Socialism with an Honest Face

The logic of the Andropov-type reformers was as follows. The socialist system as such was still better than any alternative. It had enormous reserves, and its problems were caused simply by the poor application of socialism's advantages. Following this logic, two main problems had to be dealt with: (1) the inefficiency and corruption of some of the party cadres, especially at the middle level, who had stayed in power too long, had lost flexibility, and had severed ties with the masses; (2) the widespread laziness, laxity, and dependency among people. Consequently, Andropov's reforms consisted of replacing the most odious party chiefs at the oblast levels, infusing fresh blood into the leadership of party and state, and bringing in new people not involved in corruption who were younger, better educated, and more modern. One of these new leaders was Mikhail Gorbachev.

Another ingredient of these changes was "tightening the nuts," that is, strengthening discipline by acknowledging work inefficiency and by taking absentee workers off the city streets and returning them to work. If Andropov had lived longer, we probably would have seen the continuation of this policy to throw rotten apples from the party garden and to strengthen order and discipline in the economy and among the people. On the propaganda level, it probably would have been accompanied by a "restoration of Lenin's style of leadership," which might include greater honesty about party cadres and party matters, with a renewed struggle to expose the corruption of party leaders.

Obviously, Andropov had enough information on these people while he was chief of the KGB. His leadership represented an effort to present to the world, if not "socialism with a human face," then at least "socialism with an honest face." This image included the honesty of leaders, a concern for common folk, and the struggle against the anti-Soviet elements, i.e., speculators and loafers and the "shadow economy." All this was to be done with an iron fist to keep intact the "socialist choice," the "communist perspective," and the status of a superpower. This policy probably could have lasted for another decade, but then the question of new reserves for the system and of a solution to stagnation would have arisen anew.

Another possible way of stabilizing the system to preserve socialism and give it new life, while raising the living standards of the people, lay in radical revision of foreign policy. This policy included transferring the money saved from arms reduction and using it to boost the economy. Various attempts at simply bribing the West with partial compromises—such as allowing more Jews to emigrate in return for credits, aid, and modern technology, at the same time continuing the expansion of socialism through the support of "national liberation movements"—proved futile, as detente from the 1970s has shown. Therefore, to slow down drastically the arms race and reduce those backbreaking military expenditures, it was absolutely necessary to win the confidence of the West. This required the Soviet Union to stop the spread of socialism throughout the world and to cease maintaining by force communist regimes in Eastern Europe. The propagandistic doctrine of Western and American aggressiveness had to be dropped also.

Quite possibly, this variant was considered by Brezhnev and his entourage. During his tenure, the strategic arms limitation talks were continuing, and it is quite possible—should he have lived longer—that the talks would have led to radical cuts in the mutually useless nuclear arsenals. Moreover, under Brezhnev there were signs that aid to insurgents to promote the "socialist orientation" in other parts of the world was being reduced. In 1979, when the entire world was expecting an invasion of Soviet tanks in Warsaw to crush Solidarity, this did not happen. Poland did not become another Czechoslovakia. Afghanistan, quite possibly, was the Soviet Union's last gasp to assert its imperialistic will.

In the late 1970s, it seemed to me a kind of "czechoslovakization" was possible for the Soviet Union—not through tanks but through efforts to stabilize the regime by raising the standard of living at least equal to the level in Czechoslovakia and Hungary by using the money saved from the arms race reduction. Despite keeping the power of the party and the KGB intact, a few more sausages and beer could have been offered—and the mental ferment, the grumble, and the dissidents could be long forgotten. It was not by chance that flirting with the "Hungarian model" began to include Hungarian methods of liberalizing the economy, particularly in agriculture. But something went wrong. A senile Brezhnev was not making any decisions, and there was no other active leader. Brezhnev's partocracy did not wish to hear about any reforms that interfered with the customary order.

And, in general, Soviet leaders of the post-Stalin epoch understood the danger to the system of restricting communist expansion throughout the world to save money from military expenditures and raise people's standard of living. Sooner or later such a policy would inevitably have led to the destruction of propaganda tactics such as the "enemy image," the logic of the "besieged fortress," and the need for a police state. Abroad such a policy would certainly loosen ties within the world socialist empire and threaten a chain reaction, first in the outer circle, the "world socialist camp"; then in the middle circle, the Warsaw bloc; and then unthinkably within the Soviet Union itself.[1] The Soviet leaders of the post-Stalin era understood all too well the dangers to which this path might lead.

Finally, there was a third alternative (the second choice of giving up imperialistic ambitions in foreign policy not being excluded): renouncing socialism in order to save the country and its people. This meant admitting that the socialist principles of economy management were ineffective and decaying. It also meant renouncing the dictatorship of the Communist party and moving to democracy, political pluralism, and free elections, thereby establishing these principles as the law of the land.

It is obvious that even mentioning these principles of radical reform ten years ago was taboo; it would have immediately resulted in repression of one form or another. And for a risk-taking politician, it would require much risk and years of preparation. But no less important was the question of whether the people were ready for such reforms. Or was there a possibility to prepare the public gradually for radical change and for the inevitable reforms, to avoid the sudden shock and disruption? Was it possible to draw up a plan of action, a scenario of possible events, to foresee where the first steps would lead and what the reaction of the public would be?

The answer to each of these questions is no. There was no readiness or willingness of the people to depart from socialism; to close down the Communist party; to start a multiparty political system; to move to self-government, a market economy, and the inevitable stratification of the society into rich and not so rich. Above all, nobody wanted to pay for all the reforms with food shortages, inflation, and poverty. And there were no leaders ready to assume responsibility for such radical transformations, much less foresee the course of these events.

A New Way of Thinking and the Breakdown of an Empire

Soon events started to follow this course. Having come to power, Mikhail Gorbachev began by trying all three variants of reform, yet not subscribing to any specific plan but generally following Andropov's model of "honest socialism." The very first steps of the new reformer were to take measures to improve the party image.

The "struggle with showiness," now forgotten by everyone, meant reducing the misrepresentation of facts and introducing more honest statistics into the public domain. It also provided for a somewhat more truthful press and the new, more personal style of populist leader—one "going out to the people," traveling around the country, talking to crowds, and shaking hands. Some of the old party bosses mired in corruption were replaced. This effort was probably the finest hour of the new general secretary of the party. The people were watching with growing hope and approval for the young, open, and witty leader, who, for the first time in decades, talked without a written speech and attacked the age for its showiness and stagnation. This leader did not promise paradise tomorrow, but he told it "like it is" about deficits and the other ugly sides of life, and he predicted a painful but steady recovery for the country.

Another side of Gorbachev's early policy was a "tightening of nuts," an attempt to reverse the inefficiency of the socialist economy. Consequently, "acceleration" had become the slogan of the day. Everything was to run as before, only faster, and make the old system more effective, but without radical reforms.

Public consciousness reflected that period in one of the numerous anecdotes of the time. A man running with a wheelbarrow is asked: "Why is it empty?" And the answer is: "We are in a hurry; no time to load."

The military-industrial complex was not forgotten either; a multibillion-ruble program of machine-building reconstruction was supposed to radically improve the quality of armaments. An antialcoholism campaign, invented by Ligachev and approved by Gorbachev, was supposed to be an important part of the Andropov-type "nuts tightening." It was an absurd idea, which has brought huge losses to the country, has led for many years to shortages of sugar and vodka, and has brought about an underground moonshine industry with consequent drug abuse, organized crime, and the destruction of vineyards and quality wines. And along with everything else, alcoholism persisted and even grew.

This campaign, not the most important of many reforms undertaken over the last years, was nevertheless very indicative of the style for the period; the leaders simply lacked understanding of the problem. Their blindness was marked by an inability and unwillingness to foresee the consequence of large scale governmental actions, by typical party self-confidence and arrogance, and when failure became obvious, by irresponsibility because nobody was made answerable for the huge material losses and the economic and emotional damage to personal lives. Ligachev kept portraying himself as one of the founding fathers of perestroika, yet he admonished new reformers. For Gorbachev this shady enterprise probably cost him half of his popularity.

Rather soon, though, Gorbachev understood the uselessness of beating the dead horse of the Soviet system, and he generally acknowledged the dead-end of Andropov's system with its "speed-up" slogans.

Practically from the first days of his administration, Mikhail Gorbachev attempted to circumvent this impasse by making peace with the West and ending the cold war. From his predecessors at the general secretary post, he inherited the task of negotiating with the U.S. on the subjects of strategic nuclear missiles and troop reductions in Europe and increased his chances for success by using something that had been lacking in previous decades—mutual trust among the players and, specifically, trust of the West. To win this confidence and finally to curtail the arms race and eliminate the danger of a nuclear war, he had to help the country radically change its image in the world.

It is hard to say when Gorbachev made the decision to stop promoting the communist system and class struggle on a global scale. Anyway, through numerous visits, through mutual compromises during negotiations, through his articles and public speeches, and finally through his book *The New Way of Thinking for Our Country and the Whole World*,[2] his main thesis has been delivered to the world and is now fully understood: the Soviet Union will stop supporting the class struggle outside its borders, and it is putting common humanitarian values above class, state, religious, and any other set of values. A corollary to this thesis permits the Soviet Union to curtail the spread of communism and the world revolution by force.

Gorbachev would have already earned his place in history if he had done nothing else within his six years in power except to give his address to the members of the Issyk-Kul writers' meeting in 1987, where he declared the primacy of humanitarian values over class values. This event was similar to Khruschev's denunciation of the Stalin cult at the Twentieth Party Congress. Naturally, this new philosophy was legitimized through the termination of support to procommunist regimes abroad and through the withdrawal of the Soviet military involvement in many parts of the globe. Gorbachev ended the war in Afghanistan and withdrew the Soviet troops from there. There were many other initiatives, including diplomacy trips, and each trip was turning into a greater triumph for Gorbachev, who was quickly becoming the darling of the Western public and politicians. It should be noted that bursts of admiration were not so much for the "new way of thinking" (for most advanced nations, this was normal, "old" thinking) but for the personality of a young, cultured, witty communist, who alone helped to destroy old stereotypes of "the evil empire" and reduced Soviet interference abroad. Gorbachev's image making coincided and merged with the democratic reforms occurring within the country. Gorbachev and Glasnost—this was the formula of Detente-2 that led to missile treaties, troop withdrawals from Europe, and in general to the ending of the cold war, while practically eliminating the danger of a hot war between the two blocs.

This aspect of perestroika, related to foreign policy but rather quickly forgotten in Russia, and pushed out of public memory by the domestic cataclysms, was greeted with enthusiasm at the time by the people. Public opinion polls of 1986–88 demonstrate how relieved people were at the successes of the Soviet-American arms reduction talks, relieved at how the American "enemy image" was dissolving and how the danger of a world nuclear war was no longer first on the people's list of fears and concerns. In 1987 the majority of people, according to a VCIOM poll,[3] identified the end of the war in Afghanistan and the Soviet troop withdrawal as the most important event of the year.

Driven by euphoria over the end of the Cold War, the West paid little attention to the fact that, as the "the evil empire" disappeared, Gorbachev's team had removed from the foundation of the Soviet political edifice one very important piece, and the whole structure began to list. The once shaky equilibrium was approaching collapse. In this detail was the very principle of building a world communism, for which all means were appropriate, including military force, but which Gorbachev gave up in words and deeds.

There were many steps along this path, but many things were happening spontaneously; control over the situation was to a great measure lost. Events were experiencing the "domino effect," and the imperial building collapsed. The process was accelerated by the putschists, but the matter was not just one of speed.

The world revolution and the world socialist system were advancing by conquering first with the cavalry, then with tanks, and finally with injections of dollars by the Communist Party Central Committee. The cornerstone of the world communist system was the assumed superiority of communist ideology, propagated by force; all this was similar to Nazism, whose foundation was built on the supposed superiority of the German race and its links to military force. Without these principles both systems lose most of their appeal.

Gorbachev is often accused of breaking up the Union. In reality, he was fighting for preservation of the Union, at least in some form, until his last minute in power. But the most important thing he accomplished during his short turn behind the steering wheel was to deprive communist ideology of its purpose as a controlling and dominant value system; he reduced it to the level of other doctrines, yielded first place to humanitarian values, and gave up the idea of spreading communism by force. Actually, this was what his Nobel prize was for. The rest was finished by the sun and wind. Did he really want everything to end up like this? Probably not. Could he think that it would lead not only to the breakup of the world communist system but also to disintegration of the socialist camp and eventually of the Soviet Union itself? Hardly so.

His present day critics—from the public to politicians, including both liberals and communists—are united in their criticism of Gorbachev's results: instead of a superpower with many vassals abroad, we now have disconnected splinters from a state with the strange name of CIS. And they each differ in their opinions of what should have been done.

Some are grieving about the Union and believe that it should have been preserved by any means, including the military (it was never too late to crush the local nationalists and separatists). Other critics, mourning for the Union, are accusing Gorbachev for "having lost Europe without firing a single shot." Still others believe that we have betrayed the "brotherly parties," class brothers all over the world, that we have left to fate the national liberation movements and that, in general, we have betrayed the cause of socialism in the world.

The public, namely the Russian people, are hardly concerned with world problems these days, but they do feel remorse about the Union. As always, their views here are contradictory. On the one hand, common sense and the feeling for justice lead them to believe that one cannot be forced to like one's neighbors, and two-thirds believed, and still believe, that if any republic wanted to leave the Union, it had the right to do so. On the other hand, the traditional Russian drive for unity, fortified by deeply seated imperial feelings, demands a multinational state and a powerful central government. Therefore, the same two-thirds of the Russian public have supported throughout these years the new Union treaty—more a federation than a confederation—and have approved the creation of CIS, believing it would result in some sort of union.

If Gorbachev's activities in foreign affairs were not clear to people and if some of his actions were not fully understood even by experts, his policies led to even more contradictory assessments in domestic affairs. By many he is remembered more for his endless maneuvering and attempts to reach a compromise with both the reformers and the party hard-liners; yet he seemed to lack a principled position at the most critical moments. He is accused of participating in crushing the democratic movements in Vilnius, Baku, and Tbilisi, and his role in the August 1991 putsch in Moscow is also being questioned.

No matter what disturbing events may be revealed by his biography, we are primarily interested here in the objective results of his activity during political reforms of the 1980s, which shook the country and the world. In any event, his role as a politician, who first made the decisive move toward dismantling the world communist system and who withdrew from the front line of struggle between the two blocs, is not clearly perceived by the public yet.

Revolution Without a Plan

We have seen the Union begin to join the club of civilized nations under the banner of a "new way of thinking," but it achieved little treating stagnation at home by using "acceleration" and "tightening the nuts." Gorbachev and his followers decided in 1987–88 to take the path of more radical reform within the political and economic system.

Did they have any long-term plan of reform, any comprehensive concept of transformation, or at least any ideas of the expected risk and consequences of radical reform? Probably they did not. Neither intellectuals nor the general public was aware of such a plan. If Gorbachev and his team were going to turn the country around 180 degrees by transforming it into a conventional state of the Western type with parliamentary democracy and market economy, the people were not informed and prepared for these radical changes. But very likely these long-term plans had not been thought out at all.

Beginning with the plenary session of the Central Committee in January 1987, all steps toward reform were made under the slogan, "more socialism—more democracy." By this logic, socialism, liberated from excessive bureaucracy and post-Leninist distortions, would reveal a democratic substrate and show its "human face" and would create conditions in two or three years for new economic growth using the "democratic combination of centralism and self-government." Nobody as yet could even mention borrowing Western ideas in politics or economy. As Gorbachev wrote in his book, "I would like to stress once again all our reforms we are conducting in accordance with the socialist choice; we are looking for the answers to the questions that life puts before us, within and not outside of socialism." Furthermore, "it is with thanks to the socialist system and planned economy that we can make a turn in our structural policy much easier, than under conditions of private enterprise, even though we have our own difficulties."[4] He followed this logic until he stepped down from office: to free the resources of socialism and to carry out reforms of communist ideology within the socialist system while alternating between liberal and conservative positions.

But to combine the incompatible was impossible. It is not the general ideals of Saint-Simon or Chernyshevsky, the principles of social justice and equality, the state regulation of the economy, or (what is called in the West) the "welfare state" that are being questioned here. More relevantly, could a durable Soviet socialism be preserved after seven decades of totalitarian rule, party dictatorship, and the suppression of a national consciousness? Even though it remained in equilibrium for a time, this system was doomed in the long run; Mikhail Gorbachev had destroyed this fragile balance.

Unlike China, South Korea, or other countries where modernization and economic reforms were carried out under strong authoritarian political control, it was decided in the Soviet Union to start with a controlled democratization of the society, although its strengths were not in the long-term planning but rather in its embellishments. After the failure of the economic reform of 1965, which went astray, among other reasons, because of the weakness of the democratic institutions, it was decided this time not to repeat the mistakes of the 1960s but to give people more political freedom. In fact, glasnost had become the first real accomplishment of perestroika; it reached an unprecedented level in 1988, before and during the party conference. What followed were rallies, democratic elections, formations of new parties, abolition of the Constitution's Article 6 and of party dictatorship. In general, events got out of control; the political reforms developed a life of their own.

There were endless attempts, with and without Gorbachev's participation, to put the genie back into the bottle, but all this was in vain; the system started to shake. Glasnost tore down the iron curtain and eliminated the cold war, but it also started democratization and finally put an end to the building of socialism in the Soviet Union.

Two questions are important in this regard: where do reformers come from in a totalitarian country who are not afraid to shake up the system in the name of radical improvement (or at least turn the system into something different)? And why did the system not react in time to crush dissent and stop agitation by the press and society when it became clear that they supported the departure from socialism?

First, the reformers. Those who were the true fighters for change within the regime and who did not emigrate in time were crushed by the meat-grinding Cheka and NKVD of Stalin, and they were eventually accommodated in the endless progression of gulag camps. Though few, they deserve the most respect. Here we are speaking about reformers within the socialist system who remained true to the general communist idea but who wanted to improve the system (although how can a system based on terror and slave labor be effectively humanized?). Strictly speaking, such attempts began only after Stalin's death because earlier any initiative to change things without the Central Committee's decision was quickly branded as anti-Soviet.

The first socialist reformers appeared at the end of the 1950s and beginning of the 1960s. Actually, the whole period of the "thaw" began displaying slogans like "rehabilitate the victims of the cult of personality" and "improve socialism"; phrases like "the socialist legality," "socialist economy," and "socialist culture" were common. And all this was under the control of the party. A typical reform of the period was the "economic reform" of 1963–64, and a typical reformer was the well-known economist Yevsey Liberman, whose ideas about market socialism were the cornerstone of reform. The reform was quickly curtailed, but the reformer was not shot or jailed; this in itself was progress.

The tone of ideology after Stalin was changed substantially; instead of an unquestioned subordination to the chief and his Central Committee, initiative and diversity were encouraged. This whole idea was absolutely new—socialism could be improved; it could be diversified. It became possible for a "Chinese socialism" to appear, then a Hungarian, and then a Polish Socialism. By the same logic, variations were allowed in different republics and oblasts of the Union, and subsequently the party bosses of the republics and oblasts were becoming key figures. They were allowed to experiment and were moved up the party hierarchy if they succeeded.

Most experiments and reforms were cosmetic, but the style of encouraging a nondogmatic approach to innovation took root. At this time young party leaders of this new philosophy like Gorbachev, Shevardnadze, and Yeltsin were springing up in various regions. How is a loyal party chieftain transformed into a reformer? There was no single recipe. To a great degree, all of them were children of the Twentieth Party Congress, which exposed Stalin's crimes. For many in the party, the existence of this opened abyss of terror prompted the conclusion: something must be wrong with the system that leads to such lawlessness and cruelty. Furthermore, there was the ever-present difficulty of balancing criticism of the system and a desire to change it with concern about one's well being and survival within the system.

Having expressed their disgust and indignation, the overwhelming majority of people preferred as always to stay away from politics, thereby tacitly supporting the system.

For a few members of the intelligentsia, like Andrei Sakharov, this understanding led to rejection of any offers to cooperate with the system, and they openly increased their criticism. Others chose emigration. Many other specialists, including scholars and writers, became "internal emigrants," exchanging with their colleagues over kitchen tables caustic jokes, anecdotes, and rumors about this menacing system.

There were still many who compromised with the system and continued to serve it loyally, using various justifications or conveniently forgetting, to avoid guilt, the millions who perished in jails and camps.

We will discuss later the types of personalities created by the system. At this point we need to address the question: why Gorbachev? Was there a entire cohort of moderate communists-reformers, waiting in the wings by the end of the 1970s, ready to push forward a new leader who was prepared to reform or democratize the regime radically? Or was Gorbachev a unique figure?

Sooner or later such people would have emerged. But within the conditions of the 1980s, they could appear from the position of secretary to the oblast party committees rather than from other posts. And of course, unlike the 1990s, there was no chance to move into the leadership positions for people outside of the nomenklatura, like university professors. Looking back at the period of the late 1970s and early 1980s, one cannot find in the list of provincial leaders very many candidates with the potential to be great reformers, except Gorbachev, Yeltsin, and Bakatin; the latter two were eventually brought to Moscow by Gorbachev.

Besides the luck of an oblast party boss and the support of Andropov and Brezhnev, what distinguished Gorbachev from other reformists of the period?

First, it was his incredibly flexible and skillful struggle for power, his erudition, and his broad outlook that allowed him to communicate on an equal footing with world leaders and intellectuals at home. No less important was his ideological maneuverability, a readiness to exchange an outdated slogan for a more attractive new idea—"new way of thinking." And an indispensable feature of a leader who wanted to move the masses was charisma, an ability to persuade people by appealing to them directly, over the heads of the party machinery or mass media middlemen. For this reason, it can be said that Gorbachev and Yeltsin are two great populists—with completely different styles. But both are politicians of the television age.

That type of a person striving to make socialism better, to make it humane, was rather common in the 1960s, especially among professionals and intellectuals. But the emergence of such a person within an egoistic and corrupt nomenklatura, which had its strict rules of subordination and privileges, was an aberration. Gorbachev was such a person.

At the same time it would be wrong to believe that Gorbachev wanted to destroy the system from within. Half-hearted reforms that began under his leadership were initiated jointly by a number of communist reformers, beginning with Andropov, and later by Gorbachev, Ryzhkov, Yakovlev, Shevardnadze, and Ligachev. And only Yakovlev seemed willing to take more radical initiatives.

Hundreds of books and articles have been written about Gorbachev—his tractor-driver's youth in a southern Russian kolkhoz, his

Moscow University years, his friendship with the future Czech dissident Zdenek Mlynarzh, his work as Komsomol and party chief in his oblast, his promotion to the Central Committee post in Moscow, and finally his power struggle inside the Kremlin. What was the major factor in his emergence as a reformer? When did he decide that radical changes in the system were needed and that a great leap toward democracy was necessary? We may never learn the true story.

Would there have been someone else if there had been no Gorbachev? Perhaps, but I do not see who would have emerged from that stagnant but stable system of the early 1980s.

In the history of Russia over the last century, there were a number of instances when a unique personality would emerge who could achieve revolutionary changes—for good or for bad. If it had not been for Lenin, Russian history would have taken quite a different turn. Stalin was unique; nobody else could play his diabolical role in full—neither Trotsky, Zinoviev, Kamenev, nor Bukharin.

What was accomplished by Khruschev could not be achieved completely by Malenkov, Molotov, Voroshilov, or Mikoyan. Perhaps there could be no replacement to Gorbachev in his role of fortunate destroyer of the Soviet system. And similarly, there seems to be no replacement for Yeltsin in his attempt to build a democratic capitalism on the ruins of the socialist colossus.

• • •

Another question needing to be answered that will allow a better understanding of what has happened in the USSR and Russia is why the system and the ruling elite did not realize, before it was too late, where the "improvement" of socialism was leading and why they did not stop the reformists. This still could have been accomplished in 1987, or in 1988, after the Party Conference, when it became clear that it had become a matter of dismantling socialism rather than improving it.

The younger nomenklatura, backbone of the system, had understood before the idealistic communist reformers themselves that the system was doomed. Since most of them by that time were totally corrupt and cynical, concerned only with their own comfort and not for the victory of communism on a global scale, they started to move first to make the necessary arrangements to retain their real power within the new conditions of an inevitable market economy instead of engaging in a senseless struggle with liberal democrats. While the democrats were struggling at street rallies and congresses with the rearguard of fanatical communists, the nomenklatura was exchanging its party chairs for seats in the Soviets, in the parliaments, and better still in the new business structures. They were creating foundations, commodity exchanges, joint stock companies, while they were privatizing state and party property and securing a grip on the real economic power.

Part of the party money had gone abroad, but obviously the entire nomenklatura was not going to emigrate; it is more important for it to keep control over property and the real power at home.

Russian capitalism of the end of the twentieth century is being built by a strange conglomerate of ex-party and state bureaucrats, by the operators of the shadow economy, and by the new entrepreneurs who have finished high school since 1985, when Gorbachev came to power.

• • •

Russia is in the beginning stages of developing a deideologized parliamentary society with a market economy, and its success in dealing with Russia's numerous crises will depend to a great degree on where the people perceive the country is going, what maneuvers are possible along this course, and whether there is a way back. It is very important for people inside and outside of the country to comprehend all this in order to get a clearer view of the era that had ended in 1991, the era of Gorbachev.

Could the country have chosen any other way? Could everything have been left intact, which is the viewpoint many currently have? There was no such option. The country could have dragged on for another decade, but the world was going in a different direction. Was the Chinese or South Korean alternative possible: i.e., quick economic and market reforms with tough totalitarian or authoritarian control but without freedom—and only then, some time later, democratization? Only in theory. It is true that our people were not ready for democracy, just as they were not ready for a market economy, and that our intelligentsia, with all its supposed free thinking, was not taught these things. All this is clear now. But there is a certain aspect of democracy involving human rights below which tyranny and savage despotism is allowed to exist and above which we had to rise to enter the community of civilized nations and secure Western aid, technology, and monetary credits. Therefore, the question was not whether we should have modernized first and then democratized, or vice versa. The question was whether to carry out "avalanche" democratization—or a gradual one by "squeezing the slave out of ourselves drop by drop."

If in Russia 60 or 70 million citizens had not been killed by a totalitarian system, one could theorize that it was not yet time, that it was better first to modernize the economy and raise the standard of living and only then to move toward democracy. It is true that people were not demanding parliamentarism, and a protest from within was not imminent. But any move toward progress, even in science and technology, required at least the completion of destalinization, the rehabilitation of victims of repression, and at least some loosening of central control with a bit more freedom for the people. Within the Russian people, there has gathered a critical mass of discontent with life, as well as a distrust of authorities, which is often combined with a fearful obeisance to anyone at the top—of vague feelings of injustice and wrong within the social order. All this was smoldering for a long time and could have remained beneath the surface for some time further. But perestroika and the promise of change stirred up this calm, and everything started to advance. "The process commenced," as Gorbachev said, but it went out of control, along unpredictable Russian paths.

Mikhail Gorbachev intended to cure socialism with democracy to prepare the country for a controlled market. Instead, an uncontrolled democratization with a wild market began. It is irrelevant to speculate whether the authors of reform wanted or could imagine these results. The results were simply inevitable. Russia is not China or Singapore. Although it was possible to learn from both the West and the East, Russia would inevitably produce its own hybrids, often quite ugly, in politics and economics. The Gorbachev epoch can be called a basic or preliminary democratization. It is true that new parties are still more like toys or learning devices and that the Parliaments resemble street rallies which sometime turn into street battles. Election results are often predetermined, and the people's choices are not infrequently ignorant. But the people, or at least a sizable group of them, have sampled a taste of freedom and for the first time understand that they can, at least partially, influence the course of events in their life.

The people are indignant about the imperfection of democracy; they are much more openly critical now, and this is also a kind of progress. Finally, although there is still a possibility that the arising market system may return to rigid, centralized distribution and control, a complete reversal from freedom to nonfreedom and a return to the silent society of the 1970s is impossible.

The Gorbachev era was a revolution without a plan, an experiment without a theory. Many things have proceeded differently from the organizers' expectations, and the country is falling deeper into crisis. Everything has fallen apart except for the central thing that needed to be destroyed—the powerful layer of the party-governmental bureaucracy, which would continue to sabotage reforms for a long time.

What was shaking up the system, and finally what brought it down, was not so much modernization or urbanization, or a more sophisticated public, or even the penetrability of the iron curtain—although it also played a great role. It was above all the moral decay of the system, represented by a slow but inexorable disappearance of that stratum of persons who could be called "communists-idealists" and their replacement by the "communists-opportunists" and "communists-cynics." Any system can bear only a certain level of duplicity by its members, after which the stability of the system is destroyed and any agitation from in- or outside could ruin it.

But at the same time, the basis for the longevity of the Soviet totalitarian system, besides bayonets, was its rather stable support from the people (as paradoxical as this may sound) and through the Soviet political culture created by decades of skillful application of the old "carrot and stick" method. To understand why the breakdown of the Soviet empire and its institutions occurred with such breathtaking speed, it is important to comprehend first why it lasted so long. What was the source of the political culture's attractiveness, of its magnetism (it was often called the communist religion)? Who were its parishoners and what would become of all of them after this unexpected revolution called *perestroika* turned into a long and painful period of reform?

3

The New Soviet Man

Myth or Reality?

First of all it should be said that the creation of a new Soviet type of man began from the very first days of the Bolshevik revolution of 1917, when the party proclaimed class interests to be higher than human morality. Instead of law, the party introduced the proletarian sense of justice—all is permitted to promote the victory of the proletarian revolution. The courts were replaced by the bloody activity performed by Cheka and the revolutionary military tribunals. The revolutionary workers and soldiers, like the German soldiers later on at the time of Goebbels, were emancipated from "the chimeras of conscience" for the sake of victory over the enemy. And all this was done for the sake of the "people;" the great experiment began to "raise the radiant building of communism," to create a society of justice and equality without the exploitation of one person by another.

The revolution released criminals in the manner of previous revolutions. Many of these criminals joined Cheka and other Soviet government bodies. The country was overwhelmed by a bacchanalia of "class enemy" persecutions—manufacturers, tradesmen, state machinery officials, representatives of political parties other than communist, doctors and university professors, writers and priests—all those who were labeled by the authorities or their voluntary aides as *contra* and *burgeouy* (jargon for counterrevolutionaries and bourgeoisie). By borrowing a foreign (or so-called "revolutionary") word like *expropriation,* they justified the looting of homes of those people who had conspicuous property, the professionals, the intelligentsia, and the clergy. As a rule no search or confiscation warrant was necessary; strangers came in leather jackets, pea-jackets, or greatcoats with guns and "in the name of the revolution" took away all they wanted.

Lenin encouraged the taking of hostages. For example, members of the families of recruited soldiers and officers of the former tzarist army were often held hostage to prevent desertion. Authorities were also eager to seize persons in order to ransom representatives of the overthrown regime, e.g., manufacturers, merchants, and others with money, who didn't manage to escape from the country. Hostages were periodically executed to deter the Bolsheviks' opponents or to punish those who were hesitating in their support of the revolution. Human rights were violated for decades. "We do not recognize liberty, equality, and labor democracy," Lenin declared, "if they are contradictory to the interests of liberation of labor from the oppression of capital."[1]

Mass executions of hostages were followed by another Bolshevik innovation, concentration camps, created for those accused by the People's Commissariat for Internal Affairs (NKVD), as well as for "potential class enemies," "parasites," and "alien elements." The camps throughout the vast expanses of the country became boundless reservoirs for the slow destruction of millions of people (in addition to the millions who were shot) and a source of a massive slave reserve for the "construction projects of communism."

This repression, this cruelty perpetrated to terrify individuals was only part of the tragedy being spread throughout Russia at that time by the communist authorities. From the very beginning, "the great purge" and the creation of a "new society" were plotted as a joint enterprise, a nationwide performance. In the same way that the solidarity of a criminal gang is sealed through joint responsibility for the crime and in the complicity, execution, and cover-up of the crime, the Bolsheviks tried to involve as many people as possible in the terror. This was openly stated by Lenin. "We need to encourage the energy and mass-like character of terror."[2]

In order to hold and strengthen this power, it was necessary to intensify the terror with its "mass-like character." This philosophy required that Christian values and the laws based on these values be ignored to stamp out feelings of pity and compassion, which arose from the sense of guilt and responsibility for what had been done in the face of God (this guilt was all that was left from the old, human system). For this reason, the full force of terror was directed against the intelligentsia and the clergy. Writers, scientists, and philosophers in Russia were made superfluous and arrested or exiled from the country. Within ten years, nothing remained of a literature based on free expression. The church suffered still more; thousands of priests were shot or sent to camps where they died. Most of the churches were closed, robbed, blown up, or pilfered brick by brick to use as building material. Religion and religious ethics were effectively eradicated from the culture. "There is no God!"; "Religion is the opiate of the people!"—such maxims in the mouth of the new authority sounded no less categorical or menacing than "all weapons must be turned over" or "all horses must be commandeered to the Red Army." Membership in the party and the Soviet organizations was declared to be incompatible with belief in God. Formally, the church was disestablished. But the state did not separate itself from the church completely; to insure that the remains of religion would not regenerate, the existing church organizations were controlled by Cheka and NKVD, and they used even the recruitment of some priests to inform against other priests and parishioners.

There is no data on the number of believers or regular churchgoers in the 1920s and following decades, but it is known that the religious rites were more widely performed in villages than in cities. Many people continued to baptize their children secretly, including some families of party functionaries. But as a whole, religiosity as a moral foundation of society was destroyed. The grandiose process of brainwashing began.

A well-known Russian writer, Oleg Volkov, who spent twenty-eight years in Soviet prisons, camps, and exile described the beginning stages of attack on these old, time-honored ethical standards.

> Throughout the wide expanses of Russia severe fierce winds rose and spread the seeds of cruelty, averting [people] from the spiritual quest, and demanding [they] renounce the[ir] Christian ethics, the[ir] traditions, to betray the[ir] fathers.
>
> Class hatred and inexorability were advocated. Secret denunciation and betrayal were encouraged. People with a "soft heart" were mocked. Tolerance to ideas of others, human sympathy, and kindness were considered to be unlawful. It is incredible how quickly a habit or wish to look up to the heavens could be eradicated, justice-seekers could be exterminated or thrown out of the way, and Russia could be turned into a spiritual desert.[3]

Having destroyed traditional humane ethics and religion and having created a huge repressive system, the representatives of the communist regime soon realized the need to buttress their ideological positions by creating not only an obedient and terrified citizen but also an entire society devoted to the nurturing and upbringing of the "new Soviet man."

By the early 1930s along with intensifying repressions there was created a diverse and sophisticated system to indoctrinate the people devoted to the regime. In the socialism expressed in Russia, Byelorussia, and Ukraine (as well as other republics which imitated this socialism to various degrees), the foundations of the Soviet culture and a system of ideological myths were laid down. In spite of outbreaks of resistance to the Soviet regime—starvelings' revolts, peasants' uprisings, resistance of the colonized provinces, quiet opposition to the extermination of the old Bolshevik guard—the regime had succeeded cultivating not only support for, and tolerance toward, itself but also a developing culture honoring the new religion and adoring the Leader and the party. How could it happen and why did it last so long?

How the New Man Was Molded

If the concept of a "melting pot" is widely used in American history, where the many ethnic traits of immigrants were "melted" together, creating a new, American nation, the idea of steel melting is more applicable in a Soviet context. Millions of people were being dumped as slag, and the remaining human "metal" was remelted and tempered again and again to produce the real Soviet man. Not incidentally, the famous novel of the time by Nikolai Ostrovsky was called *How the Steel Was Tempered* and described how a new man was brought up, irreconcilable to dissidents, selflessly devoted to the cause of the proletarian class and living only by faith in the communist kingdom.[4]

All elements alien to the proletariat, the slag, were being driven out or exterminated: the White army, fighting for monarchy and old Russia; the tzarist officers, even those who joined the Red Army; the clergy, disseminators of the "opiate of the people;" professionals who remained in the country and who then became the new "specialists" ostensibly trying to sabotage the Soviet construction; independent philosophers and economists and the intelligentsia in general; kulaks and middle peasants, the more skillful farmers; new Soviet military officers who represented competition to Stalin's strategists. Members of all political parties, other than communist, were liquidated as incompatible with Marxism. The most fanatic Marxists, Lenin's associates, were also destroyed, quite possibly for not approving of Stalin's style of leadership and for being blind to his special merits in the revolution.

The system of terror was not just merciless and comprehensive, aiming to destroy all real and potential opponents; it was also unpredictable and absurd. Stalin was unseating not only those who had not shown enough respect toward him in the past (and this does not even include his out-and-out opponents and critics) but also most of the bright personalities, like Kirov, whom the paranoid Stalin thought represented political competition; also, anyone was a target whose abilities evoked envy, or who just seemed to be the victim of Stalin's caprice or of some other unpredictable action. These actions were followed also by those of Stalin's satraps, who were elbowing out potential rivals and even those close friends arousing envy. In fact an old Russian joke was given new life: "beat your friends—strangers will fear." The rules of the game were constantly changing—or missing altogether. In other repressive regimes, you could earn guaranteed security by showing full loyalty in taking sides and becoming a member of the ruling organization (the Nazi party is a good example). But nobody could feel secure in the Stalin theater of the absurd, not even the closest satraps, like Molotov, Kaganovich, Voroshilov, or Mikoyan, who feared one another but were chiefly afraid of the unpredictable suspicion and rage of Stalin.

This process of terror (with the "carrot and stick" strategy) is further described by Oleg Volkov:

> The strongest new order settled solidly—based on fear and demagogic slogans—on real privileges and benefits for the triumphant ones and the janizarys. The poets and writers, musicians, artists, academicians were demanding capital punishment for people who were named "enemies of the people" by the authorities. They were echoed by the obedient choirs of general meetings. And a call was rushing across the land: "Crucify him, crucify!" Because everyone had to become either a participant of a butchery, or its victim.[5]

This constant atmosphere of fear and repression—of irrational menace, when a blow could come unexpectedly and for nothing—created ideal conditions for brainwashing on a national scale—more powerful and universal than anything during Naziism. Furthermore, one could flee Naziism until virtually the beginning of the war, while in Russia an iron curtain had descended by the early 1930s and remained until the late 1980s.

This perfect system of unpredictable terror created an atmosphere of universal fear similar to the fear of a person in a dark room or the fear of a blindfolded prisoner—unseen assault or death could come at any moment, from any direction. In this atmosphere a broad, comprehensive system of brainwashing worked quite effectively.

The culture of brainwashing was accumulating gradually, from the first days of the revolution. Writers and journalists, part of the Russian intelligentsia, played a special role in it. Some participants quickly grasped what was required from them; others, like Maxim Gorki and Ilya Eherenburg, came to their new role more haltingly. But in general they had created the greatest system of myths, the system of "socialist realism." Without the persuasiveness and attractiveness of socialist realism, the doctrine of Marxism-Leninism would remain a dull and unconvincing dogma.

For writers and artists as well as for the ordinary citizens, half-hearted admiration for the system through clenched teeth would not suffice. One had not just to act or display approval or admiration but, as with the Stanislavsky method, one had to truly fall in love with the Chief and the system and perfect this performance throughout a lifetime.

In this way were created the masterpieces of enchanting mass culture, born out of enthusiasm for the socialist, proletarian brotherhood and for the forthcoming communist future. Most creations of socialist realism, especially in the movies, can be regarded as a great Potemkin village, i.e., a fake facade like those used in moviemaking, as if the actual culture could not support the continuous promises of a bright future represented in the arts. In this context, pastoral movie idylls, like *Pig-Tender and a Shepherd* and *Cuban Cossack,* were quite normally accepted by the public as pictures of life in the near future; they were consistent with the general rhetoric of socialism depicting the best of today that will become the typical of tomorrow.

Mass culture of the 1930s and the 1940s was selling not only the material socialist achievements—the most important theme of this theater of the absurd was its throbbing enthusiasm, joy of life, and expressions of new brotherhood. A great number of cheerful, joyous songs were creating a musical background for the epoch. Many of these songs have come from the musical films directed by Alexandrov and Pyriev, who blended together Hollywood style, American jazz, and the Russian song culture. An inattentive visitor from the West could quite easily be fooled (or rather enchanted) by this atmosphere of enthusiasm, quite sincere for many Russians, and by the joy of constructing a new life.

The nation lived as if in two planes. Millions of people were disappearing without a trace in nameless common graves at the gulag construction sites, often with whole families including small children. The selection and shooting of victims most often was done at night, and these victims would dissolve forever into darkness. But at the same time, in the daytime of bright city squares, young men in white pants and shirts, and young women in red kerchiefs were marching, falling in love, hurrying to create their bright new world to the songs of Dunayevsky, Pokrass, Shostakovich, and Khrennikov.

Tens of millions of people perished in prisons, died of hunger as a result of collectivization and impoverishment, or disappeared into labor camps or into exile. But just as many people in the Soviet Union, at least in the more urban, European parts of the country, were enthusiastically building a new life, supporting the communist system, and glorifying its chief.

Indoctrination was complete: kindergartens, schools, Young Pioneers' organization, Komsomol, trade unions and party organizations, the press, literature and the arts—all were directed from one party center and all of it was aimed not just at preserving the existing system and its ruling elite but also at re-creating the population continuously and letting them enthusiastically embrace the system. A very important role throughout this process was played by the creative intelligentsia, who were motivated by the powerful carrot and stick.

The results of this indoctrination were unprecedented in scale. Ideological-cultural vaccination became conspicuous during World War II when the majority of Russia's population and those of the other republics were sincerely fighting "for the Motherland, for Stalin," and for all those ideals which helped the system develop for two decades. Therefore, it can be said that the victory of Stalin's Russia over Hitler's Germany, besides being a military victory, was also a victory of one totalitarian political culture over another. There is validity in the argument that the Russian people were fighting for the Russian land and not just for the Soviet regime—that they were motivated first of all by Russian patriotism. But other peoples of the Soviet Union were fighting selflessly too. For most of them the Soviet idea was no less important than patriotism; they were defending the land of socialism, the land of Stalin. With the Russian military victory over the Germans, therefore, one might conclude that the Soviet people loved Stalin more than the Germans loved Hitler.

In retrospect, it can be said that the greatest achievement of the Soviet totalitarian system was not only the construction of a colossal military machine, a menace to the rest of the world, but also the creation of a "new Soviet man," or at least several types of men. This explains why the system existed so long.

This new historical community of people, the Soviet people, isolated from the rest of the world, could exist for a long time reproducing itself, turning out new generations of people "dedicated to the party and the government," or at least quietly submitting to the existing order of things.

The mass culture of a totalitarian system, including the mass consciousness of its subjects, is a mixture of dogmas, social customs and taboos, and mass belief and feelings. But a few key traits of this conformist political culture could be seen in each new generation and were reproduced in subsequent generations, establishing the system's foundation and base of support.

Main Features of the Soviet Political Culture

One of the cornerstones of this political culture was faith in the communist future, a concrete version of paradise on earth without the religious mystique. Having examined historic utopias, the professional propagandists—politicians, writers, and journalists—created a rather convincing image of an abundant society where new communist people would live by the principle "from each, according to his abilities; to each, according to his needs."

The forcible liquidation of religion as an institution, the destruction of churches, and the extermination of many of the clergy had resulted in a drastic reduction in the number of religious people and the virtual eradication of religious faith from the mass consciousness. But at the same time, the spiritual vacuum was being filled to a certain degree with communist ideology which had been influenced substantially by traditional religious teachings and practices. Thus, the dream of a "next" world, of a paradise, was approximated in the promises of a more concrete, communist paradise on Earth. In a certain way, this promise was more compelling than the religious promises because propaganda was stressing a real attainability or realization of this ideal, which would be achievable for the next generations under communism. Khruschev had gone as far as to promise in the 1960s that "the present generation of the Soviet people will live [under this] communism." One could hardly resist believing those promises.

This progress was just the kind of hope needed to cope with hard, half-starving life in the provinces. And for many dwellers of the larger cities, there was visible evidence of this possibility for rapid progress. Despite the great personal losses to industrialization (mainly at the expense of the peasants), despite millions of victims of collectivization, and despite the failures of those noisily advertised five-year plans, the nation's progress compared to mostly rural prerevolutionary Russia was substantial and conspicuous. Although the rise in the standard of living was modest (food rationing ended only in the late 1930s), industrial progress was impressive.

At the May Day parades the regime was demonstrating the powerful military machinery; aircraft and dirigibles were plying the skies. Other examples of progress were also evident: icebreakers were crossing the Arctic expanses, tall modern buildings were being built in the cities, giant factories were being erected in the newly born industrial centers, tractors were being driven in the fields and automobiles in the towns—and all this was raising enthusiasm. Even though industrial achievements during the early five-year plans and the subsequent restoration of industry after the war did not result in much material gain to the average person, this technological attainment still gave hope that within twenty or thirty years even more progress could be achieved. And impressive things were achieved: the completion of the White Sea–Baltic Sea canal and other canals connecting rivers, a Palace of Soviets the size of an Empire State building with Lenin's statue nearly half that size on top (only the war had stopped this insane project, already under construction), and after the war a leap into outer space before any other country—all these accomplishments were feeding the hope that the communist paradise was achievable and achievable very soon.

The obvious utopianism inherent in the communist dream did not have the same appeal to those who managed to escape the meat grinder of repressions. Rather, this idealism applied more to the generations of the 1930s, 1940s, 1950s and at least in part to the 1960s. During those decades the Soviet political culture had turned into a stable self-reproducing system resulting in a Soviet civilization with its own faith and a distant beautiful goal.

Most people in other countries lived with a faith in a better future for their children or in some other world. But here the bright future was being born out of the present, was becoming its extension, and was constantly being used to boost programs of selfless work through personal enthusiasm. A poem by Mayakovsky quite vividly described this mentality. Workers at one of the construction projects of a five-year plan had paused to rest in the mud and rain and began dreaming: "In four years there will be a garden-city here." The poem became required reading in all the schools.

Another important conception connected with the new Soviet man was a deeply rooted idea of universal equality, brotherhood, and collectivism of the Soviet people, in contradistinction to the individualism of the West. These beliefs were widely spread in the 1930s and the 1940s, and were less prevalent from the 1950s until the 1970s. This habit of mind contributes to the current nostalgia among older generations for the Soviet past. Many of them are quite ready to forget their dream of communism, but they will not give up their recollections and regrets of the difficult but brotherly life from their past. Almost every person over forty has some memory of a student or workers' hostel, of service in the army (excepting, of course, the prison-like atmosphere in military barracks of the last two decades), of communal apartments, which one shared with a number of other families, where all lived as one huge family, sharing common joys and concerns.

Camaraderie of this type, based on common work or joint living circumstances or military mission, is typical of people in many countries. Perhaps an additional closeness was more characteristic of Russians, especially in villages, where large families lived together in one house and where these situations were being transferred to urban living environments. But in Soviet times this spirit of camaraderie had acquired a special meaning. First, the communist ideology tried to eradicate personal initiative (and by extention the exercise of human rights) in favor of class interests. And collectivism was a reliable tool to curtail the development of personality and independent thought. A collective was an ideal environment for bringing up social conformity, political like-mindedness, and devotion to official ideology and the ruling party.

Inseparable from the idea of universal brotherhood was the doctrine of equality as a chief social value. Of the three slogans of the French Revolution, equality and brotherhood were understood literally by the people and were emphasized in every possible way through propaganda and through the culture. Freedom, on the other hand, was described in casuistic Marxist terms as a "realized necessity," or was interpreted for the Soviet people as a freedom from bourgeois exploitation (with limitless and uncontrolled exploitation by the state).

Equality and brotherhood were also used to describe relationships between groups of peoples, such as the brotherhood of Soviet peoples and the proletarian internationalism. Racial equality was being intensely promoted and took root very deeply, especially between European and Asiatic ethnic groups. For a period of time, in the 1920s and the 1930s, the traditional Russian antisemitism diminished only to reemerge after the war under the official label "rootless cosmopolitism."

Social, racial, and ethnic equality; the ideal of a brotherhood of people; collectivism—each with its political and propagandistic motifs, and official exaggeration and boasting—remained characteristic traits of the Soviet mentality for almost a half-century, until the 1970s, and were spread among a substantial part of the population.

Collectivism was successful and mutual aid was natural for many; these practices were accepted by new generations of youth. At the same time the totalitarian system also established limits for collective brotherhood and disinterested aid. There were well-understood taboo zones, which one did not enter. Someone from a collective disappears; another person does not show up for work or appear in class or return to the hostel. No need to ask; "the competent organs" know. The organs declare a brigade member or office worker "an enemy of the people," a spy, or a Trotskyite. "It must be so; the organs know best. Let us condemn the renegade and close ranks."

Collectivist logic and conformist mentality became inherent parts of the mass culture. An equal share to everyone; live as others do; do not stick your neck out—and everything will be all right. Those who did not follow this folk wisdom often disappeared. Taught by fear and by feelings for self-preservation, people knew where not to look. If one did not know about the privileges of party bosses, one would see few differences in income distribution, with an engineer getting little more than a blue-collar worker. In the 1930s workers of heavy industries, metallurgy, machine building, and aircraft construction, could afford to spend a summer vacation in the Black Sea resorts. The sea, the surf, the white clothing—these miniparadises were becoming a reality for a sizable number of workers and employees in large cities, at least for those who did not perish in the camps. In the late 1930s the growth of the standard of living in the cities became quite visible, along with expressions of equality and brotherhood.

It was as if the country was living on two levels, one on the surface and one deep inside the catacombs. There were crowds of singing enthusiasts, marching jubilantly across broad Moscow squares, enjoying life more and more and rallying around the chief and the party. And at the same time millions were perishing in Lubyanka basements or were being taken in endless freight trains to the north and the east to die a slow death in the camps.

Ordinary Germans stated after the war that they did not know about the concentration camps. Ordinary Soviet people were also saying they did not know about gulag. Collective amnesia is a powerful tool of a totalitarian system and is used as a means to insure its self-preservation. But while in Germany it worked for only fifteen years, in the Soviet Union it continued for fifty years. The system had effectively implanted into mass consciousness both the idea of equality and the notion of collective responsibility and collective irresponsibility. These feelings are quite enduring, and many people keep remembering how nicely they lived in the past—"as one family," poorly but joyfully. And what about the responsibility for killing millions of innocent people? "It was a difficult time;" "the country was in jeopardy;" and "sacrifices were inevitable."

Authoritarian traits within the masses also became the bulwark of a system of complete totalitarian control. It was based on traditional Russian peasant authoritarianism and then was intensified by the system to create complete submission to the totalitarian regime. The traits of the authoritarian personality are discussed in detail in chapter 6. The observations here will be restricted to the political consequences of this Soviet mindset.

The authoritarian personality and mode of thinking with its system of hierarchical attitudes applied to interpersonal relations, family life, and social and political behavior was transformed during the Soviet era into a conscious and unconscious love of the chief and the party, into esteem for, and fear of, any official, and into a servile submission to authorities. Authoritarianism was also the basis for a major theoretical principle of all party and government activities, "democratic centralism." In practice, it refers to the submission of a minority to majority in decision making and the suppression of criticism, dissent, and political factions within the party (not to mention a general ban on other parties). Violation of these written and unwritten rules led to the removal of offenders from official positions or even removal from the party with the label of "enemy of the people" (and possible disappearance).

Participants who followed the rituals of the authoritarian game in great detail were promised a transfer to a higher level in the Soviet hierarchy with all the attending benefits (concealed, of course, from a public enjoying its brotherhood through equality). Gradually, a layer of fat, comfortable, devoted party functionaries, closed to the outside, was created—the nomenklatura, the backbone of the totalitarian system.

Besides cementing this order of nomenklatura, authoritarianism was also the glue binding the mass political culture together, the glue between citizens and the system. By and large, the people meekly accepted as natural total state control over all aspects of life, and the state was personified through use of numerous small and large forces, the most significant of whom were the Leader and the Party. The deification of Stalin had reached its peak in the 1930s, 1940s, and the

1950s, and the party, led by him, became not simply the most formidable institute of power but also something spiritual—a nonmaterial creation surrounded with a halo. In the communist lexicon, it was called the "spirit of the epoch."

Even the arrested "enemies of the people," out of whom the Cheka torturers beat confessions of crimes which they did not commit, or who were forced to slander other innocent people—even they were being forced to "disarm before the party." The victims were compelled morally to cooperate with the butchers in the name of a supreme being, the party, and to love that which supposedly continued to unite them. This practice was similar to that found in some other countries, where an investigator appeals to a criminal to repent in the name of God. This perverted mentality of Soviet hangmen is very vividly depicted in Eugenia Ginsburg's novel, *In the Whirlwinds of History*.[6]

Military and athletic parades on Red Square and in similar sites in other cites were obviously well-rehearsed propaganda shows similar to the Nazi torch marches at the Nuremberg stadium in fascist Germany. But at the same time, the mass exultation at these festivities and rallies, with their enthusiastic praise of the chief and the party, sincerely illustrated the people's respect and admiration of, and their voluntary submission to, the totalitarian system, and they helped the system to claim victory in World War II, despite the nation's great human losses.

Human losses during the war, amounting to 27 million people by modern estimates, effectively meant that the nation had lost a huge number of the male population from its most vital age groups with consequent genetic damage to the nation for decades to come. But even more destructive to the genetic stock of the country were losses of 40 to 60 million from the active population (possibly even more) because of the repressive regimes of Lenin, Stalin, and their successors. It severely damaged the demographic structure of the nation and adversely influenced the mental abilities of the people, who performed at a lower educational and cultural level.

But no less negative was the impact of this bloody experiment on the national character, reinforcing and creating anew the slave mentality. This condition was not just a servile submission to authorities or speculation about sources of irritation to officials. It was a slave mentality, people born into slavery who loved their cage and their guards and who praised the party and the system not with gloomy desperation but with sincere joy and adoration: "Caesar, those who go to their death salute you!"

In accounts of the Nazi mass culture, I have not found poetry or songs dedicated to Himmler, the Reich's chief hangman. Indicative, however, for the perfectly absurd mass culture of the Soviet totalitarian system was a poem dedicated to the number one butcher, NKVD chief Beria. "The kids are having a great time; it's a feast for Pioneeria, They say, 'He'll visit us today—Lavrenty Palych Beria'". (The author is unknown, but probably perished in camps, as did the author of another famous Pioneer song, "How good it is to live in the Soviet land!" who was listening from his prison cell as Young Pioneers were marching in the street singing his song.)

"O tempora, o more!" In what times we lived! And all this is still very much alive in many people: for some, it is just a sweet nostalgia for the days of youth; for others, it represents a somewhat altered Soviet morality and behavior; for still others, it is like a faded tattoo—a lingering regret for the strict order that had disappeared following Stalin's death.

Apart from the 40 to 60 million people who are not accounted for and who probably perished during Stalin's inquisition, much of the rest of population was turned into a conformist body supporting the system, believing in the imminent coming of communism, united with the proletarian-communist brotherhood, and feeling a sadomasochistic love for the system and its chief.

With this grim picture of the processes of Soviet mass political culture formation (and of its product—the new Soviet man), we can trace how the combination of these traits created different types of Soviet thought and determined their relationship to the system and their political feelings. Actually, there was the whole spectrum of attitudes—from full support to hidden disapproval and hatred. These types of Soviet thought need to be examined to better understand (1) the structure of this mass support for the earlier system, (2) the undermining of this support during perestroika, and (3) the nature of this source for democratization and its transition to a market economy presently and into the future.

Types of Soviet Mentality

The types of political thinking within the Soviet mass culture can be arranged in five main groups, groups which had been formed largely in the 1930s and which existed in some way or another until the beginning of perestroika. Throughout these years, some of them had become predominant, while others were diminishing in size; and what we chiefly have today are the transformed Soviet types of political culture. They did not disappear; nor were they replaced by the "new people," the "democrats," but under the conditions of social or economic upheaval, the authoritarian or other traditions of the Soviet political culture would surface again.

Because available terms describing this unique political culture (and the types of personality characteristic of it) do not exist, and because the terms of western political science, such as liberal-conservative or right and left, cannot be applied here, we must create our own expressions for these types. Thus the main types of the Soviet political consciousness are: "true believers," "collectivists," "conformists," "cynics," and "critics."

In identifying these types we will be using mainly a combination of three major traits of the Soviet political culture: the communist faith, adherence to the idea of social equality and brotherhood, and Soviet authoritarianism. Actual persons possess other psychological and moral qualities, which make the real palette of people's characters as diverse and bright as in any other country, but for political typology we can isolate these main qualities for our discussion.

The True Believers

This ideal type, created by the Soviet system, is its pride and chief source of support. In such people true faith in the imminence of the communist paradise harmoniously combined with adherence to the idea of equality of all people regardless of race, nationality, or sex. Equally important is the idea of "leveling" or a readiness to serve the collective unconditionally, with an equal share of the benefits going to all (and, of course, to serve the highest collective of all, the working class). And what followed was an unqualified submission to the proletarian state in all its branches, and a selfless devotion to the party and the chief. These people made up the backbone of the Red Army in the civil war; they helped build the huge plants of the first five-year plans; they fought with dedication during World War II; they reconstructed a ruined country after the war by developing the virgin lands; they went to the country to help the backward kolkhoses.

In most respects, they were fanatic adherents to the communist idea both in its principles, its major deeds, and through their habits and relations with people in daily life. Irreconcilable and merciless to followers of other convictions, they were ready to fight the class enemies physically and took part in the dispossession of kulaks and the eradication of other "enemies of the people." These people were enthusiastically joining the Cheka and other repressive organs. Many became party and government functionaries at all levels, and many, unlike the current trend, remained personally and materially disinterested and did not accumulate any real possessions out of their service to the party and its ideology. The main protagonist of Nikolai Ostrovsky's novel, *How the Steel Was Tempered,* is a good example of this type.

The degree of idealism and fanaticism in such people was limitless: "one's entire life should be devoted to the struggle for the proletariat victory and for world revolution." There was no room for a private life. Moreover, "the pursuit of happiness" and other humane traits were eradicated and scoffed at and were considered an unpardonable Philistinism. However valuable these people were for the system, it was not possible to turn most of the populace into such types—human nature what it was. In its ideal form, this type was more typical of the civil war period; when life was assuming a more normal course in the 1930s, a more modest idealism and fanaticism became more widely spread.

The number of these personality types during the Soviet era can only be approximated. The share of the "true believers" throughout the population during the prewar period was probably near 20 percent.

The "true believers" perished in great numbers during World War II, and thereafter their percentage within the population declined. Presently, this type is more represented in the older cohorts; they remember their heroic Komsomol youth when they approved of everything done by the party, including its struggle with the "enemies of the people" and its glorification of Stalin. Their numbers can be assessed, on the basis of the polls, at 5–7 percent of the population.

Collectivists

The most common and widely occurring type of Soviet man was the "collectivist–communalist," which arose in the 1930s and represented a majority of the population that had escaped repressions for a few decades. For these people, faith in communism was more abstract, more theoretical, and they were not ready to die for the world revolution. In general, they were less fanatical.

The emphasis in their thoughts and beliefs was not so much on the future, which deserves dying for, but rather on equality and today's communal brotherhood, on joyous labor for the good of the collective, on egalitarianism as a moral philosophy of life. Such a person was ready to do everything for a comrade or a fellow-worker; he rejected individualism, egoism, personal enrichment, and material accumulation, as well as dishonesty.

If we forget for a moment that these people comprised the huge crowds marching past the House of Unions where infamous Moscow trials of the 1930s were held and demanding death sentences for renegade "Trotskyite dogs," this type can earn our respect with its many idealistic humanitarian features. In fact, some of these traits, including diligence, modesty, and self-restraint, were cultivated by the system in these people and were acquired from Christian morality.

Being left to its own devices, this type gradually underwent a mellowing process, especially in peaceful times, by helping to reduce class hatred and by helping others to acquire these same humanitarian traits.

To discourage this practice, the system had to rouse the Philistines constantly with fictitious enemies; the system was forced to create new subjects that would perpetuate class hatred. These included the never-ending succession of Trotskyites, Right and Left deviationists, foreign spies and saboteurs, bourgeois nationalists, "cosmopolites" and Zionists (i.e., Jews), and finally "ideological saboteurs," people revering the West and disseminating Western bourgeois culture. The fantasy of the well-paid propagandist had no limit, and there was plenty of space in Siberian and northern gulag camps for their victims.

The roots of the "collectivist" type can be found in the Russian peasant community where they were nourished by certain Orthodox features and by traits of the Russian national character described in literature. These traits include openness; an inclination to create stable, friendly ties; and collectivism. All this acquired a special hue within the Soviet political culture. The foundation of this communist brotherhood was the production brigade—the main cell of society and a kind of new socialist family. This brigade culture as a carrier and a custodian of the moral standards of society continued to develop until the 1980s. Its last refined version was the so-called communist brigade, a prototype of the future communist community and organization of labor in our days. Brigade members not only assisted each other in their work but also cared about such things like education, the upbringing of children, and the treatment for alcoholism, and they helped solve many problems of daily life. This last attempt at mass communist indoctrination to create this "new man" has disappeared without a trace, but the idea, developed to an absurdity, is quite typical of the collectivist mentality for this Soviet type.

For a half-century the ideas of the communist collectivism and brotherhood were held, in varying degrees, by a great number of people, and this type was widely spread throughout the Soviet political culture. Their numbers comprised 30 to 40 percent of the population from the 1930s to the 1960s. Then it began to decline, and in the 1980s and the 1990s it fell between 10 and 20 percent, with this type spread mostly throughout the older cohorts, especially those above forty years of age.

Silent Conformists

Despite its attempts to increase the number of collectivists, the system could not halt the growth of the nonparticipants or passive bystanders—the silent, cautious conformists. Many of them occupied the lower rungs of the social ladder and included peasants forced to join kolkhoses, some blue-collar workers, and especially the middle layers of the urban population working within the trades and services. They had learned well that this system does not forgive any deviation in political behavior or life style. Because they lived in constant fear, they had developed a stable habit of noninterference in politics, a kind of tacit yet fearful support of the system. Their philosophy could be summed up in simple maxims: "we are simple people; all this is none of our business;" "we don't want to know what's going on above." Quite possibly this was the most successful way to survive. Nonparticipation in any organization and the avoidance of any movement up the social ladder was fraught with less danger than exposure from overreaching and the subsequent fall from grace. The system could not turn these people into active builders of communism. Many of them were hiding a deep enmity of the system, but a deeply rooted fear was preventing them from an active opposition against the system.

These people were generally alienated from society. They had lost any hope of somehow influencing the course of events in society, and thus they became nonpolitical. This group had stubbornly resisted indoctrination during Stalin's rule. They also kept away from politics during this period and refused any attempt to understand radical reforms. They simply did not believe in the possibility for ordinary people to influence state policies. Apolitical people exist in every culture. But the magnitude of this type of person in the former USSR is the result of decades of totalitarian cultural domination, and it has produced both the active supporter of the system and the mechanical man who thoughtlessly follows its orders. The number of these people can be assessed at 30 percent during the Soviet era and is probably closer to 40 percent within the last decade.

Cynics

From the standpoint of social and political transformation, the most interesting type is the "communist-cynic." This is the very powder charge that has shattered the system from inside.

The Revolution was carried out not so much by high-minded idealists—there were more of them in the Socialist-Revolutionary party than among the Bolsheviks—but rather by opportunists who were thirsting for power for personal gain and who were using the communist slogans as a cover for robbery and corruption. But their behavior was still considered an aberration, and sometimes such people were exposed and prosecuted. Their style and practices were contrary to the political cultural philosophy in the 1930s and the 1940s: there were still quite a few idealistic and disinterested leaders in different positions of power.

The moral decay of the elite was started by Stalin with the creation of a layer of nomenklatura in the 1930s—a closed order of party and government functionaries highly paid and with many fringe benefits. Members of this group were not unassailable; they could easily be arrested and shot on the basis of a report. But their moral principles concerned the higher authorities less and less, and various vices, such as heavy drinking and personal corruption, were either pardoned or punished by a simple transfer to another position within the nomenklatura.

While the system was praising modest, industrious, and selfless idealists, it was in practice rejecting the most uncorruptible and honest, those who were becoming the purist white crows among the more corrupt bureaucrats. Officials not taking bribes were pushed out because they represented a danger to the others. Despite what the propaganda slogans said, the nomenklatura system was forging its own hero, a corrupt careerist devoid of moral principles skillfully using the communist rhetoric for camouflage.

The range of colors was quite wide here. There were individuals who retained, for their emotional balance, some general faith in the theoretical advantages of socialism and in the theoretical possibilities of building communism. Their justification of privileges and corruption was: "Nothing doing; everybody lives that way. It's better that a good man, like me, keeps this place than some rogue." Or "I'm doing a lot for people, working day and night. I deserve some special privileges."

A second type of reasoning was not without self-reproach: "Of course, this is not what Lenin has adjured to us—all this servility to rank and to bribes. But what can I do; you cannot jump over your superior. The main thing is not to do vile things, not to report on others, not to act meanly stepping over the corpses."

A third type of logic went this way: "Because you have leadership talent and other abilities, you should use them and get what you deserve, whatever the system. And if the system is inflexible and does not value people, you have to protect your own well-being."

Finally, the simplest explanation was: "All this talk about morality is fairy-tale-like; utopia you have to grab, as everybody else is doing."

Gradually, the management of the country throughout governmental, party, and ideological levels fell into the hands of this very type of person. Their numbers grew from around 10 percent before the war to 20 percent in the 1980s. Most importantly, the "communists-cynics" have replaced the "true believers" who gradually faded away. We will speak about the decomposition of the regime later, but here we have to mention one more type in the Soviet political culture, its critics.

Critics

The people identified as critics were not those persons who were fighting against the communist regime or who even managed to emigrate. Rather, they were those who, critical of the regime, stayed in the country after the revolution and the civil war (or who were born and grew up under the Soviet regime).

By reading the documentary literature on the tragic history of Russia in the twentieth century, one can get the impression that the repressions of the totalitarian regime were aimed at its opponents. The situation is more complicated than that: the majority of the victims were not its enemies or active opponents. Many were its enthusiastic supporters. Moreover, among the victims were Lenin's associates, organizers of the Revolution. And if some of those, fallen prey of the great terror, were conscientious opponents of the Stalinist totalitarian regime or became opponents inside Lubyanka cells or the camps because they grasped what was going on in the country, the majority still continued to believe, even behind barbed wire, in communist ideals, in the advantages of the Soviet system, and in Stalin's genius. If they had doubts about the system, they more likely focused on a few specific defects in the system than on the whole structure. Their criticism of power, ideology, or the political system was selective and did not undermine the foundations of the system.

Some of these "selective" critics believed that the enemies had crept into the headquarters of the NKVD and that Stalin did not know what was going on. Consequently, many were attempting to write to

Stalin, secretly or openly, to tell him of the betrayal of the "organs" while praising the party and the chief. Others thought that there had been a departure from the Leninist standards after Stalin's seizure of power. Therefore, if the party got rid of the dictator, things would straighten themselves out along Leninist lines, to the benefit of socialism and communism. Finally, it became clear to many that, although the party and government system had been criminal, the ideas of socialism and communism were not responsible for this phenomenon. This attitude helps explain why, after Stalin's death and with the beginning of prisoner rehabilitation, many of them joined ranks to help build the very system that had thrown them behind barbed wire and had exterminated millions of others.

Within a totalitarian regime, such a loyalty to its ideas from these victims is probably unique in Soviet history. And the paradox is that the system has not used, to any significant degree, this store of faith and loyalty.

Finally, at the opposite end, or rather outside it altogether, were people, both in the first postrevolutionary years and in the 1960s, 1970s, and the 1980s, who understood fully the criminality of the totalitarian giant and were trying to fight it secretly and openly. Unfortunately, this subculture of protest, which became more visible in the 1970s, was successfully neutralized by the colossal repressive and propaganda machine and did not influence mass consciousness in any appreciable way. Also slight was the influence of Western information sources and emigration policies, whose materials were seeping through the Iron Curtain. The system was decaying from within but in a peculiar and slow way.

As mentioned earlier, the detachment of true believers, of idealistic fanatics, which could provide a real foundation for the totalitarian regime, was decimated during the war, became thinner from repressions, and eventually grew old and was not replaced with young recruits in the postwar years. The system was relying on the more modest collectivists who could also provide enough honest leaders and economic managers dedicated to socialist and communist ideas. But the totalitarian system could not be honest with itself and allow this more civilized path of history. Despite partial destalinization and the ending of mass repressions in the mid-1950s, growth of the nomenklatura continued at an accelerated rate. Still enjoying mass support of the population, the system was rejecting the most able in favor of the most loyal and was driving out honest idealists, who could compromise the mutual secrecy of corruption, favoritism, and personal stealing.

After the regime underwent some liberalizing during the thaw of the 1960s, entirely within the limits of communist doctrine, the decay of the ruling elite intensified again in the 1970s. Corruption, hypocrisy, and open enrichment of the party-government nomenklatura had become more conspicuous and defiant. Former party idealists were now transformed into a ruling, wealthy elite, which sharply contrasted with the very modest living standard for the rest of the population. And this perception was fortified by the caricature figure of a senile Brezhnev, decorating his shining court-dress coats with new medals.

The situation was fraught with paradox. The decay of the ruling elite, quite obvious to the population, was eroding the support of the system from the collectivists, the middle-age cohorts; it was contributing to the growth of an entire generation of alienated youth; yet it had not stimulated powerful forces of protest, resistance, or reform. Hatred of the ruling elite had not led to mass rejection of the system. The stagnation of ideas and a growing layer of apolitical, cynical, and conformist functionaries guaranteed relative stability of the system for a long time.

4

The Winding Road to Democracy

For the first time in Russian history, radical changes in the country are being carried out, and the mass public is able to participate. Public opinion has become significant in replacing leaders, choosing the political direction, and reforming the national economy. In this period of dramatic change, especially political change, with persistent attempts to return the country to communist rule, the political orientations of the public are tremendously important. At this point, certain questions need to be asked. Will the next putsch attempt gather enough public support? To what extent do liberal-democratic reformers enjoy public backing? Is a "soft" reversal to the Soviet-communist regime possible through the democratically organized elections of procommunist leaders, or political adventurers of other orientations?

Political views of the Russian public in the mid-1990s are primarily products of the totalitarian communist past. For some people it is a creed, for others vague idealistic leanings, for even others nostalgia for the past. Even those who actively promote new democratic ideas often profess a mixture of liberal and conservative views. Whatever the situation, attitudes of the past are the material from which new beliefs and values are molded.

Features of the Past

When we consider the political culture of Soviet society, derived from the seventy-year-long totalitarian epoch, its most salient feature is an all-embracing fear of repression imposed by a system that punishes any departure from the dictated behavior and thinking. This fear is sometimes conscious and sometimes not. The system used the entire spectrum of rewards and punishments to maintain obedience, and at one end of this spectrum, there always existed—and it was common knowledge to everyone—labor camps, prisons, and even physical extermination. An important element in the general atmosphere of totalitarianism was the suppression of any independence of thought, initiative, or self-expression. People felt pressured to repeat official communist ideology and to spread it to all spheres of education, science, and culture. All mass media were controlled by the party and state; and this allowed them to perpetuate the communist myths and standards of thinking and behavior. Under such conditions, it is difficult to speak of the existence of a public opinion that could differ in any way from the official ideology and the system of prescribed values imposed on the mass consciousness.

Within a major part of society, this condition resulted in an impetuous, Pavlovian enthusiasm about everything happening in the country and in servile support of the regime and any agency of power. In other parts of the populace, the suppression of personality by the system created a distrust of any opportunity for personal participation in political decision making, and this lack of confidence, combined with feelings of complete alienation from power, led to widespread political apathy. The absence of individual and collective opinion, the innate fear of being conspicuously different because of personal beliefs, the fear of differing from the official point of view—all these attitudes are persistently revealed even in the latest public opinion polls where 20 to 30 percent chose safe positions, i.e., "difficult to answer" or "no answer" responses when answering socially meaningful questions.

Another important quality of Soviet mass consciousness at the start of the reform era is the extent of its conformist psychology. This condition has resulted from a deep penetration into mass consciousness, especially Russian, of the authoritarian type of personality, way of thinking, and behavior. In a study carried out by the author in 1990 on crime-related problems, several questions similar to Adorno's F Scale were asked. Results showed that 63 percent of Russian citizens believed that strictness and discipline are the most preferable methods for raising children; 52 percent considered "strong leaders to be able to do more for the country than all the laws and talk," while only 30 percent disagreed with this statement.[1]

One of the consequences of this psychology is what is often termed by liberal critics *Russian slave psychology*: a readiness to obey or follow the authorities' directions, the concept of passive subordination, and a belief in the ideological unity of the crowd or class led by wise leaders, such as the party chiefs. A further element is the indelible Russian and Soviet belief in a "kind Tsar;" it includes the idolization of monarchs and other rulers and is illustrated in many writings about Lenin and Stalin. This respect, to a lesser extent, suffuses in modern mass consciousness and is displayed, for instance, in the extreme reactions to the abilities of the leaders of perestroika, Gorbachev and Yeltsin—from adoration one month to mass disapproval the next.

This lack of practice in forming opinions, especially political opinions; the suppression of any strong, alternative political movements or doctrines; the lack of any forum for mass discussion of these topics on the eve of perestroika—all of this resulted in the absence of an alternative weltanschauung. What the populace also lacked was the very idea of a range of political orientations or a belief in political self-identification, whether left or right, liberal or conservative. The only theoretically possible identification was to be communist or anti-communist, and the second position was punishable under the law.

The pressure of official ideology and its system of values, supported by the strength of the state and its repressive apparatus, created the impression of a total and unshakable faith of the people in official dogmas. The lack of feedback through independent media or public opinion surveys concealed any breaches within the dominant political culture. The absence of any opposition corrupted the power elite and carried the rituals of communist faith to absurdity. At the same time, it created a sort of underculture of hidden grins, irony, criticism, and protest and developed as an evolving parallel political culture.

The growing hypocrisy, the double standard of the leaders and the official propaganda (which became increasingly more evident in the 1960s and the 1970s) was responsible for splitting the mass consciousness—at least within the more educated part of the population—into a public behavior and then into a separate, private behavior, the former with points of view conforming to official standards, the latter with behavior and opinions for "oneself," "among one's own company," when there was no control. That "false bottom" of mass consciousness, a counterculture in fact, was based mostly on the refusal principle (a parody of the official party line). Furthermore, it was underground and had no opportunity for the free exchange of ideas through the media, except as published in a limited number of dissident publications.

This consciousness of denial was especially evident just before the introduction of perestroika and stood in total contrast to the famous and most accepted communist myths.

One official cultural myth—the moral and political unity of the Soviet people—continued to coexist with the progressive fragmentation of society. Social division was forged by the antagonistic interests of different groups: the bureaucracy with the nomenklatura at its head, professionals and intellectuals, skilled workers and technicians, collective farmers, retail trade personnel, underprivileged and homeless people, the growing criminal and marginal groups.

Another myth—the indestructible friendship of our peoples and the creation of a new historical unity of peoples—was in fact being undermined by the reality of ethnic and religious misunderstandings and conflicts, and by the regional divisions of the country, divisions between European and Asian parts, between the center and the provinces, between the cities and villages.

In spite of a widely spread belief in the communist paradise (and the continuous support of the socialist attitudes and slogans), formation of the "new Soviet person" or "the young builder of communism" was far from complete and was quickly becoming another myth, bearing little connection to reality. The supposed high socialist morality, which was to embody such an ideal person, turned out to be, in real life, responsible for the destruction of traditional humanitarian standards and values. Along with the proclaimed collectivism of the Soviet people, the very opposite was developing, "rude individualism" and selfishness. Despite the claimed negation of private property and the Western "cult of ownership," there was growing materialism and even "conspicuous consumption," and these features are described in more detail in chapter 6.

The mass culture, with its officially inflated enthusiasm and its glorification of communist virtues in songs, movies, and literature, was contradicted by real life and was helping to create a counterculture of protest and a new folklore for the "criminal" underworld, which had become contemptuous of power and bitter at the hypocrisy of officialdom.

Finally, a significant part of this unofficial subculture has become evident in the creation of spontaneous surrogate political views: an amorphous dislike of power, feelings of alienation from power and society, distrust and political apathy, dissatisfaction with life, the absence of civil rights, and the impossibility of changing anything within the conditions of one's existence.

Nevertheless, immediately before perestroika Soviet society was relatively stable. The repressive mechanisms were still strong and the protest movements had not yet formed because they lacked channels for expression and had no alternative goals or programs. As we will see later, each of these features of the Soviet mass consciousness played a role in the formation of public political views, which were precipitated rather unexpectedly by radical political reforms—our "great leap forward" toward democracy.

Political Reforms and the Public

The era of reform, formally initiated in 1985 when Gorbachev came to power, began slowly within the economy and the Russian political life. At first, traditional methods of screw tightening—making the existing system work more efficiently and giving it more honesty and humanity—were used, with a mobilization of mass initiative and some restraint exercised by the nomenklatura dictatorship. Only in 1987 was the slogan "more democracy—more socialism" launched. This slogan suggested important democratic reforms but only within the boundaries of the socialist system. It was taken up rather quickly by the intelligentsia, and an unprecedented political discussion began. It was approved by the party chiefs and helped lay the groundwork for the Nineteenth Party Conference, which took place in June 1988. The debate in the media and among the public, organized by the party, soon got out of control: it raised many questions that had been taboo for a long time. These questions or complaints included criticism of the existing one-party system and dictatorship of the Communist Party's top echelon, the uncontrollable power of the bureaucracy, the absence of free elections, suppression of the opposition and informal political movements, the absence of any separation of power, a poorly developed system of laws, the defenselessness of citizens before the state and especially at the hands of the repressive KGB. These things were rather openly discussed in the national media for the first time. The conference itself was broadcast live on television, and its speeches and resolutions determined the development of future political reforms. But the process of democratization extended its control beyond Gorbachev and the party during the next few years, and it began to follow its own logic under pressure from the intelligentsia and from the influence of rising mass political views.

Although liberal intellectuals readily seized upon this unique historical opportunity to move the country towards democracy, the revelation of these horrifying facts from the past (with the newly proposed radical reforms) produced a deep cultural shock within the rest of the public, the full consequences of which are too early to assess. But some observations on the process of this formation of a mass political consciousness during the period can be made.

First, the atmosphere of glasnost, the charismatic and populist personality of Gorbachev, and the appearance of new liberal political leaders like academician Andrei Sakharov caused a growth of interest in politics, especially as communicated through the media. For instance, according to the Soviet-American study, "Television and Society," conducted at the end of 1989, the news programs of Central Television were viewed most widely; 58 percent of the respondents said that they were most interested in them. Sociopolitical programs took second place with 31 percent; musical and entertainment programs each received only 28 percent.[2]

Glasnost roused the people. Politics became an exciting show, with bright personalities appearing on TV programs. Sharp criticism of the system and of the drawbacks of Soviet life from the screen was consonant with the public mood, unlike the practice of leader and party glorification in the past. Participants in the rallies and congresses were openly challenging the party bureaucracy and party leaders. But together with this outside interest in political performance, there could be heard appeals to open politics to the public or, in Gorbachev's words, "take the human factor into consideration," let the people take part in governing society. This basic idea of democracy, power to the people, received the quick general approval of the public. Welcomed also with equal enthusiasm was the idea of free elections with alternative candidates. Ninety percent of potential voters participated in the first democratic election in the spring of 1989. Sixty-one percent of them believed that real power should be given to the Congress of Peoples' Deputies, elected by the people, and only 10 percent wanted power to remain at the "party-governmental apparatus" level.[3] As will be mentioned later, these representative bodies of democratically elected legislative power were the first to enjoy broad public confidence, which they kept longer than other institutions of power.

At the same time, this newly acquired public faith in democratic elections and parliamentary bodies was shaken rather sharply by the reality of local elections where, multiple choices of candidates notwithstanding, the election was often won by the figure from the party bureaucracy because he had support of the party apparatus, money, and easy access to the press. This is further reflected in the decrease of voter turn-out in recent elections everywhere.

In general, interest in politics during the period of perestroika has grown substantially. For example, during the presidential election in July 1991, VCIOM poll data showed that 54 percent were interested in politics "greatly" or "to a certain extent."[4] Here "the glass half full" should be viewed optimistically since, during the Stalin or even the Brezhnev era, "to be interested in politics" meant not minding one's business, to be doing something reprehensible and dangerous, because "to be engaged in politics" was the business of the heads of the party, the government, and of party activists—and all the rest were simply to follow and demonstrate "mass support."

But at the same time, even in 1991, only a limited number of people were actually taking part in political activity of one form or another. Although membership in the Communist Party had fallen from 10 percent to 4 percent of the adult population over the previous three to four years, according to poll results (with 8 percent reporting that they had resigned from the party), there was no matching gain by any other party; indeed, less than 1 percent had joined the numerous new political parties. Another 3 percent reported in the polls to have donated money in support of political movements or initiatives, 4 percent to have taken part in strikes, and 6 to 7 percent in mass rallies and demonstrations. Besides elections, this latter activity was the most popular form of political participation.

In 1992–93 political participation grew very little. For example, in May 1993 only 1.5 to 2 percent of people polled were members or active supporters of political parties and only another 1 percent were supporters of other public organizations. At the same time 24 percent of the population were ready to take part in a rally to protest price increases and shortages of consumer goods.[5]

The public's political apathy continued to grow in 1993, despite the fact that 1993 was represented by a high degree of political struggle in the upper echelons of power, including the confrontation of President Yeltsin and his conservative opponents in the Parliament and the October putsch attempt. To further illustrate this point, in May 1993 a referendum on the president and his socioeconomic policy took place and 65 percent of potential voters cast ballots; by December 1993, only 54 percent participated in the parliamentary election, as compared to 75 percent who participated in the presidential election of 1991 in Russia.

The old system of ritual political participation—in the Communist Party, in the official trade unions, or in the Komsomol—had fallen apart, although a new mass network of civic society had yet to be formed. What was left in the public perception of political activity were mainly two alternatives: parliament or riot, i.e., elections on the one hand, or mass rallies, demonstrations, strikes, and acts of civil disobedience on the other, with almost nothing in between.

Attitudes toward different forms of political participation showed themselves in two polls: one before the first election in 1989 and the other at the end of 1990. At the preelection survey, perceived effectiveness of different forms of participation was measured. Answering the question "what forms of political participation can most strongly influence decision making by organs of government?" 49 percent chose "articles and interviews in the press, radio, and TV"; 38 percent (to the utter amazement of survey organizers) chose "participation in public opinion polls;" 15 percent indicated "working in the Party, Komsomol, and labor cells;" 14 percent chose participation in election campaigns and elections; 13 percent chose "participation in mass rallies and demonstrations;" and only 7 percent mentioned taking part in activities of "informal groups and associations," the nuclei of new, noncommunist parties and movements.[6] After the election, respect for parliamentarism grew, and the elected Supreme Soviets enjoyed much trust until the upheavals of 1991.

The emphasis on "direction action," and not on elected institutions or the network of civic society, became even clearer in the poll of December 1990, when it was shown that public dissatisfaction with the economic crisis had grown considerably. Answering the question, "how will people react to the worsening of their economic situation during the transition to a market economy?" respondents chose the following positions: "they will express their protest speaking to one another"—35 percent; "there will be mass disturbances and riots"—35 percent; "they will protest at rallies and demonstrations"—24 percent; "they will be working harder to increase their income"—12 percent; "they will appeal to the press, to their deputies"—only 9 percent.[7] The level of confidence in the Supreme Soviets was still high at the time, but the public did not view these organs of power as their instrument to affect policy.

These are the reflections of more general and widely spread perceptions of low political effectiveness and the resulting alienation of people from power and society. Several surveys probed this topic. For example, a study by the author, "Institutions of Power," in September 1989, has revealed the following attitudes of the public: 45 percent believed that "people whom we elect to organs of power soon forget about our needs and are not concerned about the public's view of their performance in office;" 31 percent believed that "the leadership is a special group of people, an elite, who don't care about us;" and only 14 percent believed that "our organs of power are part of the people, that they have the same interests as the rest of us."[8]

The Soviet-American survey in December of the same year asked the question about whether the elected Peoples' Deputies "from your district" will be true to their campaign promises. Thirty-one percent answered in the negative, 37 percent positively, and 31 percent did not answer.[9] The somewhat higher assessment here than in the previous poll can be explained by a greater level of confidence in "one's own" candidate than in the remote political elite or the power circle in general.

To measure the level of alienation in the author's 1990 survey, several questions were asked that are often used in American polling practices for that purpose. (A more detailed description is in chapter 6). Thus 81 percent agreed with the statement that "everything is so uncertain these days that it seems anything could happen;" 65 percent supported the statement that "everything is changing so quickly thee days that it is hard to decide which are the right rules to follow." For 82 percent it seemed that "many things our parents stood for are going to ruin before our very eyes;" 74 percent thought that "the main problem today is that most people really don't believe in anything."[10]

The Crisis of Confidence

To what extent do these feelings of general alienation translate into political alienation, into a perception of isolation from governing bodies, or into mistrust of the institutions of power and their leaders? Five years of polling have supplied some data on the dynamics of trust and confidence of the population in both the traditional institutions of power and the new centers of power created by perestroika and the new elections. The monitoring of public confidence in political institutions and leaders can of itself provide a good political history of the "Gorbachev era" or the "Yeltsin era."

The combined results of various VCIOM polls, probing public confidence in important institutions of society, are presented in table 4.1. As a rule, the questions contained three gradations of trust: "complete" or "high," "average" or "partial," and "low" or "lack of confidence." Although for a proper assessment of trust it is better to know all three levels or, even better, to have a "feeling" thermometer (in the case of some institutions, such as the Communist Party, even "partial" confidence would be considered a serious disloyalty verging on treason in

Table 4.1
Public Confidence in Various Institutions: High Level of Confidence
(in percentage)

Institution	1989			1990			1991			1992		1993	
	Mar.	Aug.	Dec.	Jan.	Mar.	Sept.	Mar.	July	Sept.	Jan.	Sept.	Jan.	June
Supreme Soviet (of USSR)			45	39	34	24	3	17	28	3			
Supreme Soviets (of republics)	40	32	28	26		40	32						
Supreme Soviet (of Russia)			20	19	19	49	33	34	45	13	6	10	9
USSR Council of Ministers	26	14	34	31	23	15	10	10	20	9	2	12	18
Local Soviets	17	16	17	19		18	12		17	10		11	12
Communist Party	37	22	23	19	16	11	10	8	12	4			
Trade Unions	21	16	20	18	16	16	11	19	16		5		13
Komsomol	16	11	10	10		7	5						
Armed Forces			44	40	35	36	40	33	41	45	30		39
Militia	14	10	25	21	22	20	19		19				16
KGB			38	35	32	29	23	19		17	12		20
Courts			22	22	21	20	16		21				16
Religious Organizations	17	22	30	31	37	43	43	29	39	38			
Mass Media	37	30	36	42	41	35	22	20	36	20	19	25	26

Note: Values for USSR until July 1991. Values after August 1991 for Russia only.

the recent past), in the interest of brevity we report only "high" or "complete" confidence percentages.

A quick glance at the data from table 4.1 might suggest an extreme volatility of views, of dramatic swings in public confidence. Although volatility is certainly an important feature of emerging Soviet political consciousness, there are also some discernible trends at the level of trust.

One trend reveals a large drop in public confidence for institutions associated with the departing totalitarian system, specifically, those institutions that are symbols of the communist bureaucracy: the Communist Party, the Komsomol, the Union Ministries, and the Council of Ministers of the USSR. These old idols have fallen in public esteem with little chance of any recovery.

Yet the new institutions that emerged on the wave of perestroika, glasnost, and democratic elections have enjoyed a rather short honeymoon period of high trust. For instance, the Supreme Soviet of the USSR, the first organ of the government of reform, has quickly disappointed voters with its inability to solve the pressing problems of society and to deal with the endless factional struggle within its ranks. Other elected Soviets, including the Supreme Soviet of Russia, had similar fates. The Russian Supreme Soviet reached its peak of public confidence, 49 percent, in the summer of 1990 but had lost much of this confidence by the end of 1991, when the Union collapsed and Russia appeared as an independent state. And later its public confidence continued to decline until its dissolution and the outbreak of the second putsch in October 1993. Even the very symbol of glasnost and democracy, the uncensored and mainly liberal press, lost most of the public's confidence in 1991 when it became the messenger of bad news. Finally, even the religious organizations, having remained the symbol of the spiritual and cultural renewal for society, lost some of their popularity because they were unable to stop the deepening crisis.

Interestingly, a relatively high level of trust was given to the army, the KGB, and law enforcement agencies, even though confidence in them was also declining. For example, in the first half of 1991, a high level of public confidence was enjoyed by the strange combination of the Supreme Soviets of the various republics, the army, the KGB, and organized religion. Apparently the public, having no clear political orientation, was ready to grasp at any straw and appeal to any force that seemed capable of stemming the tide of crime or stopping the country from sliding into economic chaos. After the August 1991 putsch, the army and KGB lost much of their public support (the KGB, of course, does not exist in its previous form), but the tendency for the public to put its trust in any political force or organization pretending to play the role of savior still exists.

It is interesting to compare the level of trust in different regions of the ex-Soviet Union. In general, the more conformist and pro-Soviet views were from the Middle Asian republics and Kazakhstan, even though, in these republics, these views had to coexist with growing nationalistic, Islamic, and separatist feelings. The western regions of the nation, forcibly annexed on the eve of World War II, never fully submitted to the occupation and preached the communist ideology through clenched teeth. These areas include the Baltic states, Moldova, and western Ukraine. Feelings of separatism never abated there and eventually developed into active separatist movements during perestroika. The Slavic republics of Russia, Ukraine, and Byelorussia occupied a middle position in their political views.

Despite a different history, culture, religion, and tradition, the transformation of political views in these regions was experiencing similar fluctuations or cycles, and the lack of confidence in the totalitarian institutions showed up everywhere. Table 4.2 demonstrates how the confidence level looked in different republics at the beginning of radical political changes in a September 1989 poll.

As evident in the table 4.2 statistics, the level of confidence in all organs of the Soviet power and communist institutions was twice as low in Estonia as it was in Russia and Kazakhstan; yet, trust was much higher there in the religious organizations and the new informal associations, the rudiments of noncommunist political parties.

At the same time, in all three republics, as well as the rest of the Soviet Union, confidence had increased in the new, more democratically elected parliament and in the press, the vehicle of glasnost and democratic ideas.

In general, a crisis of confidence existed with respect to most institutions in government. The old totalitarian system of power had disintegrated, and its remaining fragments were out of favor with the public: the new parliamentary or representative system of governing bodies is still in the process of formation but is already losing public confidence due to its lack of effectiveness—the only criterion on the minds of a people looking for the light at the end of the tunnel of crisis. And the structure of a future civic society—the new political parties, mass movements, and associations representing and defending interests of different social groups—is still being born and as yet has

Table 4.2
Public Confidence in Various Institutions: No Confidence
(in percentage)

Institution	Average (for USSR)	Russia	Kazakhstan	Estonia
Media	10	6	11	5
Supreme Soviets (of Republics)	15	12	15	14
Informal Associations	26	26	41	10
Local Soviets	27	28	22	26
Communist Party	31	28	23	55
Religious Organizations	33	31	50	22
Labor Unions	36	33	29	53
Ministries, Council of Ministers	38	35	32	50
Law Enforcement	41	33	42	66
Young Communist League (Komsomol)	50	48	41	81

Source: Nikolai Popov, "Attitudes Toward the Institutes of Power," VCIOM report, Sept. 1989.

no mass support from the public. As a result, people are ready to engage in all forms of protests, "direct action," demonstrations, or civil disobedience; they are ready to support any political demagogue or opportunist who promises a quick salvation for the country and an exit from its economic chaos. For example, in January 1992 after the liberalization of prices, 30 percent of those polled had considered spontaneous mass public actions in the streets against the rise in prices quite possible, and 39 percent were also ready to go out onto the streets to join such a rally.[11]

Similarly, in October 1993, 38 percent said in a poll that they were ready to participate in a rally against price increases and a falling standard of living. Forty-seven percent believed that "spontaneous mass protests against economic policy of the government" were quite probable. In October 1993, on the eve of the second putsch, 26 percent were ready to take part in a political rally or strike in support of either Yeltsin or Khasbulatov's Supreme Soviet, even though the public got tired of endless political struggles at the top.[12]

This readiness materialized during the Moscow events of October 2–3, 1993, in mass clashes of the demonstrators with the police, which led to the bloody putsch attempt. Whatever reasons its leaders had, there was enough fuel for such actions in the agitated masses, who were ready to riot.

The End of a Dream

The state of confusion, worry, and lack of perspective on the part of the Soviet public was reinforced by the vacuum of ideals following perestroika. The absence of polling data on this sensitive topic from the previous decades does not allow us to speak with confidence about the public belief system in that period. Available information shows that, on the eve of perestroika, the communist ideal had faded substantially or, at least, belief in the rapid construction of the communist paradise, promised by Nikita Khrushchev to occur "within the life of the present generation of the Soviet people." The utopianism of such forecasts occurring even in the remote future was obvious to many people and often was treated ironically, especially by the youth. But, at the same time, many aspects of the socialist doctrine were still widely present in the mass consciousness. Among them were: equality in the distribution of material welfare and wages (i.e., a leveling process); reliance on the state (statism) as opposed to private initiative and dependence on one's own efforts; the primacy of the interests of society, class, and the collective over the interests and rights of the individual; the belief in democratic centralism or majority rule that suppresses the rights of the minority, including national and religious groups. Many of these folk-socialist views continue to exist in today's mass consciousness and are closely interwoven with more recent democratic beliefs.

With the beginning of reform, glasnost, and liberal criticism of the crimes of the communist regime, these changes led to noticeable alteration in mass ideology, at least as widely verbalized. Those who once hid their revulsion of the regime and its ideology could now reveal it openly; those who hesitated to take a stand against socialism now chose more radical attitudes, under the influence of the liberal press, that were critical of the communist and socialist ideals. But the views of most of the people can be described as an eclectic mixture of socialism and democracy.

The first political poll in February 1989 revealed the following public assessment of the causes of the country's economic problems:

1. Economic problem are caused by the errors of the past—57%

2. Our difficulties are inevitable consequences of the socialist economic system—18%
3. Perestroika is responsible for economic hardships—4%
4. Other answers / difficult to answer—21%[13]

This assessment was made at the dawn of democratization on the eve of the first democratic election. Half a year later after the elections and the dramatic First Congress of Peoples' Deputies, the polling showed a somewhat different and more detailed picture of public notions of societal problems, including their causes and possible cures (see table 4.3).

These attitudes were quite typical of the Soviet mass consciousness during that early transition period and continue to be typical to the present. Some people are still emphasizing the necessity of democratic elections for the parliamentary bodies. Others, in a populist manner, are hoping for benevolent rulers or demanding fast replacement of the old guard. Yet others want to get rid of the remains of the command economic system. And some still want to carry out economic reforms within the socialist system. At one extreme are the true Stalinists and at the other the proponents of a market economy and democracy.

An important characteristic here is a certain split in mass consciousness: on the "theoretical" or abstract level many are still supporting socialism or hesitate to abandon it completely; but on a pragmatic level concerning concrete actions in politics and the economy, many of these people support measures that amount to actual democratic reforms and transition to market economy.

It should also be noted that there is a split or contradiction of a different type in the mass consciousness. Many people have—often on a deep psychological level—statist notions, expectations of help or provision for everything needed to be supplied by the state, with related ideas of communal equality and the distribution of income. These notions exist as self-evident beliefs, basic feelings, and predispositions, and they often coexist with attitudes or statements about democracy and radical political and economic market reforms on a theoretical level.

Often these people, especially the intelligentsia, have understood the process of democratization mainly as a departure from Stalinism and as cleansing socialism of the birth pangs of dictatorship and terror, trying in reality to build a socialism "with a human face" and create a market with "socialist regulation" and a concern about people. Many of them, shocked by the continued hardships of the people and the multiple crises generated by radical reform, would like to return to

Table 4.3
Public Attitudes about Societal Problems: Their Causes and Cures
(in percentage)

Attitude	Average (for USSR)	Russia	Kazakhstan	Estonia
Everything will be resolved if everyone works honestly.	37	40	32	31
Because the people who have led us into this crisis are still in power, this old leadership should be replaced completely.	30	28	27	38
The administrative-command system is still intact. We need to change not just the leadership but the whole system.	30	35	15	39
Everything will be resolved when the true representatives of the people are elected democratically to top positions of power.	25	27	16	35
Economic reform should be carried out with the real involvement of leasing enterprises, cooperatives, and small individual businesses.	16	16	13	25
Socialism in its present form has exhausted its capabilities and shown its ineffectiveness. Only private property and a market economy can lead the country out of its dead end.	14	11	12	40
Only a firm hand and iron discipline, as existed under Stalin, can save us.	8	9	18	2

Source: Nikolai Popov, "Attitudes Toward the Institutes of Power," VCIOM report, Sept. 1989.

Note: Respondents could choose several items.

planned production and distribution; they want more socialism but still theoretically support democratization.

Thus, in answer to the question, often asked in the VCIOM polls, "which economic system is better?" 33 percent preferred the one "based on state planning and distribution," while 39 percent picked a market-oriented economy with private property and 28 percent could not give an answer.[14]

More specifically, attitudes toward socialism or toward a "socialist choice"—the one supposedly made by people in the Revolution of 1917, a definition often used in political discussions—were surveyed in the survey, "New Constitution of the Russian Federation and Public Opinion," conducted in the spring of 1991. Respondents were asked: "We often hear that our country has made a 'socialist choice,' while others claim that we still have to choose our own way. Which of the following statement would you rather agree with?" (See table 4.4.)

Thus the true opponents of socialism comprise 38 percent, the true supporters, 28 percent; the rest can be characterized as hesitant or without a clear-cut ideological orientation, which is quite typical of a large part of society in this transitional period.

It is indicative in this regard that many prefer to describe the most desirable path for the country's development in nonideological terms. They avoid such words as *capitalism* or *socialism* and apply vague expressions like "the Swedish model." In the same poll, while answering the question, "what kind of society should be built in the Russian Federation?" 29 percent chose socialist, 3 percent capitalist, and the majority of respondents, 56 percent, selected "a society which combines the best features of both socialism and capitalism [as implied by the Swedish model]." Twelve percent did not answer the question.

Discussions about the future of socialism in the country, with its merits and shortcomings, as well as use of the term in political struggle, have diminished substantially after the breakup of the USSR and departure of the Communist Party as a ruling party in 1991. But the discussion about the usefulness of radical reforms and the wisdom to depart from socialist principles continues. On the eve of the parliamentary election in October 1993, a majority of 58 percent believed that the "introduction of a market economy is wrong for the future of Russia," while 42 percent considered it a step in the right direction.[15]

This finally brings us to the notion of communism or the "communist perspective" in the popular mind. After a seventy year indoctrination of children and adults with a devotion to an idea, only 18 percent were able to state during the poll that they knew what the communist

Table 4.4
Public Attitudes about Socialism
(in percentage)

Attitude	
Socialism has demonstrated its failure, so we should follow the path of modern countries.	38
Even with its shortcomings, socialism still remains the most just political system, and we should keep building on it.	20
What we have created is far from socialism; we have to start over.	19
Our people chose the socialist way in 1917, and we shall not turn away from it.	8
Difficult to answer.	14

Source: Nikolai Popov and Roussina Volkova, "The New Constitution of the Russian Federation and Public Opinion," VCIOM report, Mar. 1991.

perspective is all about. Fifty-five percent did not know and another 27 percent could not answer the question, which suggests that they lacked sufficient grasp of this idea. A more practical question, "can communism be achieved at all?" was answered in the positive by only 13 percent, doubted by 22 percent, while 47 percent were sure that communism can never be built.[16]

A survey in March 1993 conducted by the sociological service VP headed by Boris Grushin has uncovered similar attitudes. Fifty-seven percent did not agree with the statement that the "communist system is most suitable for Russia," 21 percent agreed partially, and 22 percent did not answer.[17]

An indication about attitudes concerning the communist idea is also revealed in the public's ratings of the most important problems as measured by VCIOM since 1991. "Departure from the ideals of socialism" was mentioned as the most important problem by only 4 percent in 1991 and less than 2 percent in 1993.[18]

Attitudes about communism are also reflected in public assessments of the Communist party and its possible role in the future. During the "prehistoric" years, confidence in the party had declined considerably. Further exposure of the party's crimes and its role in the Soviet totalitarian system has led to the mass withdrawal of people from its ranks in 1990–1991, especially after the first putsch, when the party was almost banned. In 1993 by the decision of the Constitutional

Court, party activity was allowed again. By this time the emotions connected with party banning had subsided, and the public was considering new roles in society for the communist parties, which emerged after the court decision. These new assessments were recorded by the VCIOM polls.

In February 1993, 30 percent thought positively about the renewal of activity for the Communist party in Russia; 36 percent rated it negatively, with 34 percent having no opinion on the issue.[19] The one-third rating this renewal positively should not necessarily be considered supporters of communism. Rather this group represents a mixture of communists and people with democratic orientations—those who believe that the banning of any political party is incompatible with the democratic principles being introduced in Russia. Therefore, a significant number of opponents of communism have advocated, by court decision, the return of communist parties to the political life of the country.

Twenty-two percent of the public also believed that, in the future, the communist party "can become a real political force." Forty-four percent disagreed, and 34 percent did not have an opinion. Answering a more direct question about whether the Communist party "can in the future return to power," 17 percent responded positively, 45 percent thought it impossible, and 38 percent did not have an answer.[20]

These assessments of the political potential of the Communist party have noticeably altered, just within the three dramatic months of spring 1993, when opponents of reform (with a sizable participation from communists) made an attempt to oust President Yeltsin, stop the reforms, and take control of the press. Failure of these attempts and the defeat later of these forces at the referendum of May 25 have again reduced the level of support for communists and their chances for returning to power. In May 1993, only 15 percent believed that the Communist party can, in the future, become a real political force in Russia, and only 11 percent thought the party could return to power. Sixty-two percent believed it was impossible, and 27% did not answer.[21]

These evaluations of the potential role and influence of the Communist party remained valid until the December 1993 parliament elections, where communists received 13 percent of the votes or a third place after Zhirinovsky's Liberal Democratic party and the bloc, "Russia's Choice," headed by Gaidar.

Thus on the ideological level, adherents to the socialist way for Russia's development make up one-third of the population. Furthermore, those who have become disenchanted with socialism do not automatically become adherents of capitalism. In trying to move away from the accepted ideological stereotypes, they either reject any political ideology because the political culture lacks visible alternatives or, without knowing exactly what it means, they actually support the logic of convergence, which was bitterly opposed and criticized by the former official propaganda.

Important aspects of mass ideology at the time of radical reform were the public views on democracy. In general, the majority still supported one type of democracy or another. An "improved" socialist democracy existed during the Gorbachev era. After the party conference of 1988 and the election of 1989 discussions about democracy began as such, without using the adjective, "socialist," and soon it even became popular to contrast democracy with socialism. The majority of the population enthusiastically accepted the transition to democracy, until price increases and the sharp drop in the living standard occurred in 1992.

The upheaval of radical reform and the breakdown of the economy have caused a sharp increase in criticism of the reformist government for promoting transition to a market economy and democratization, and this has resulted in a decline in popularity of the very concept of democracy. Vacillation about this subject will continue, and instead of just demonstrating approval or disapproval, the people's attitudes between these conditions will be even more important.

A large group, from one-quarter to one-third of the population, considers authoritarian rule or dictatorship to be the only solution to the crisis in Russia. For instance, a week before the dissolution of the Soviet Union in December 1991 (and four months after the democrats' victory over the putschists), 34 percent believed that the army could act with the support of a "strong hand."[22] In January 1992, 24 percent advocated dictatorship at the onset of rising prices; in October this number rose to 32 percent.[23]

In February 1993, during the period of galloping inflation and Yelsin's intense power struggle with the Congress of People's Deputies, 26 percent of the population believed that "the only way out of the situation . . . is to set up a rigid dictatorship." Fifty percent did not agree with that position, and 25 percent did not answer.[24]

On the eve of the referendum in April 1993, the number of dictatorship supporters had declined somewhat to 21 percent and remained at that level through the summer.[25] In September 1993 on the eve of the second putsch, the number rose to 26 percent with 47 percent disapproving, and 27 percent unable to answer.[26]

What did the people want the dictatorship for in the first place?

Table 4.5
Attitudes about Radical Reforms
(in percentage)

Attitude	
Buildup of chaos and muddle in running the country	61
Growing uncertainty about the future	46
Crisis in national relations	38
Deepening of economic crisis	37
Weakening of national defense	24
Growth in the public's political and economic activity	8
Revival of ethnic pride	7
Beginning of the nation's economic renovation	7
Expansion of political rights and freedoms	6
Strengthening of the nation's international positions	6

Source: VCIOM survey, Mar. 1993.
Note: Data applies to reforms beginning in 1985.

What illnesses of the society did they wish to cure with authoritarian rule? First on the public's list of concerns for the previous five years were economic problems—shortages of consumer goods, inflation, and a general breakdown of the economy. A second major concern among the public was crime, which threatens millions of people.

Another way to assess the public's condition and response is in their evaluation of the reforms' results, which began in 1985. In March 1993, during a period of intense debate about the future of the country and the causes of current crises, the following assessments of the "main results of perestroika and radical reforms" were made.[27] (See table 4.5.)

It is in the context of these problems that the public approach to the choice between "democracy" and "order" should be considered. Even though these concepts are not antithetical, the public often contrasts one with the other. Subsequently, people chose "order" as most needed by the nation. For example, in October 1993, after the second putsch, 76 percent opted for "order," as compared with 11 percent who would have preferred "democracy," with 14 percent having no answer.[28]

The eagerness to support dictatorship, therefore, is related to the desire to put things in order within the country and to attain some

Table 4.6
"What can most rapidly secure order in the country?"
(in percentage)

Answer	
Strict observance of the laws.	54
Rapid implementation of economic reforms.	26
Emergence of a new strong leader who will take care of all our problems.	23
Concentration of all power in the country in one person's hands.	14
Elevating the role of local governments; creation of local public bodies of law enforcement.	8
Handing over of all power to the army, police, and other security forces.	6
Control over the sources of power by the public through regular referenda.	6

Source: VCIOM survey, Apr. 1993.

protection from crime. Table 4.6 evaluates the ways order can be achieved in the public's mind by examining the question "what can secure order in the country most rapidly?"[29] One-quarter of the population prefers various undemocratic forms of governance, each offering a different emphasis as a temporary measure to solve the crisis.

Somewhat differently, authoritarian feelings were expressed by one-third of the public, who believed, after the referendum in May 1993, that the "activity of the Soviets of all levels should be suspended and a direct presidential rule introduced." This was the opinion of 37 percent, while a minority of 26 percent were opposed and 37 percent did not have an opinion.[30] Many of these people can be considered more democratically oriented because they were struggling against the Soviets, including the Supreme Soviet, which were controlled by ex-communists. In other words, for many people authoritarian methods of running the country (or even dictatorship) are acceptable as long as they are directed against, in their mind, "others" or negative or destructive political forces. However, in relation to themselves and to their social or political strata, they demand democratic treatment.

Another measurement of the degree of democratic orientation in the public mind is the level of tolerance for the opinions of others, specifically, for those public utterances which are not shared by the

Table 4.7
"Should people with the following views be allowed to express them publicly?"
(in percentage)

Controversial view	Yes	No	DK/NA
People believing that Lenin as well as Stalin is responsible for repressions			
Express their views in newspapers	48	43	9
Speak on television	48	44	9
Be allowed to teach in colleges	39	49	12
People advocating inferiority of some nations			
Express their views in newspapers	18	75	7
Speak on television	18	75	7
Be allowed to teach in colleges	14	78	8
People standing up for the legalization of prostitution			
Express their views in newspapers	24	71	5
Speak on television	23	72	5
Be allowed to teach in colleges	23	72	5

Source: Boris Grushin, Nikolai Popov, Ada Finifter, George Gerbner, and Ellen Mickiewicz, "Television and Society," Soviet-American Study of Public Opinion, report, Mar. 1991.

majority of people, which are considered questionable, or which evoke the condemnation of many. The assessments of such responses were made in the Soviet-American study of 1989.[31]

Political tolerance was probed in this survey in a question about Lenin and Stalin's responsibility for mass repressions. At the time, criticism of Lenin had just begun. The prevailing views among the public supported Lenin's democratic principles, which they believed had been violated by his followers, especially Stalin. Two other questions dealt with national equality and prostitution. (See table 4.7.)

As the data show, more tolerance is expressed in relation to political views and less tolerance for moral-ethical issues. Utterances or beliefs stated in the press produce less disapproval than if those beliefs were expressed in a college classroom. In general, the level of tolerance is rather low, which suggests undeveloped democratic feelings and orientations.

The level of tolerance correlates well with age and education; the younger and better educated people have a higher level of tolerance. For instance, 67 percent of people with a college education supported people with questionable political views expressing their ideas in the press, 52 percent with a high school education did so, 45 percent with an education level of 8–9 grades, and only 26 percent with less than seven years of schooling.

But even greater differences existed between people in different regions of the USSR. This is how they responded to the question whether to allow people with controversial political views to speak on television.

	Russia	Estonia	Georgia	Uzbekistan
Yes	51	70	78	28
No	42	20	17	62
Difficult to answer	7	10	5	10

After the dissolution of the Soviet Union, this trend continued. The public in Russia and in other parts of the former USSR opposed dissemination of views unpopular among the majority and was not ready for a plurality of opinions at the marketplace of ideas. Low tolerance in combination with authoritarianism will continue to be used as the basis for molding mass attitudes about the new economic and political realities for some time to come.

People's conceptions of democracy generally are quite vague and often seem to combine incompatible ideas. On the one hand is the support for representative bodies of government, for the multiparty system, for free elections, for the primacy of the individual over the state, and for the inviolability of human rights and freedoms. On the other is the support for social "wage-leveling," egalitarianism, the nostalgic demand for a powerful "democratic" imperial state, the restoration of the union, and for support of populism, anarchy, and "democratic centralism," a principle which presupposes the subjugation of a minority to the majority.

We can identify the following trends in the mass political consciousness or political orientation of the public during this transition period from the results of the various political polls conducted from 1988, which was the beginning of regular polling in Russia.

Although the population has undoubtedly been shaken from its slumber by the period of radical political and economic reforms, a significant portion, between 15 and 30 percent, is utterly excluded from political life. Still unpoliticized for a variety of reasons, they understand nothing of what is happening around them, and, what is more, they have no desire to understand. Roughly 20 percent have a zero interest in politics. Twenty to 30 percent of those polled consistently "have no opinion" or "cannot answer" questions pertaining to economic or political issues on a national level.

The rest of the people try somehow to come to terms with what is happening in the country. They can be divided into three groups. The first group is composed of antidemocrats, proponents of various forms of totalitarian or authoritarian rule. Of them, 7 to 8 percent are patently Stalinist. The authoritarian group comprises no less than 15 percent of the population, but this percentage could easily grow to include one-third of the population in a time of crisis. For example, on the eve of the abortive coup in July 1991, nearly 30 percent supported the proposed ban of all political parties, mass meetings, demonstrations, and strikes—pending the emergence of the country from crisis.

The second group is made up of the proponents of market reform who lean toward democratic development. They amount to 20 percent. The bulk of this group consists of people with a higher education.

A question needs to be asked in this regard. Why was it primarily older cohorts and not the youth that were most active in the movement toward democratization? First, the political and moral crisis of the system, with its stagnation, mendacity, and hypocrisy, has led to the destruction of moral codes and values within the society in general and, specifically, among the youth. In the 1970s and the 1980s, the majority of the young people sensed that the only opportunity to move ahead in life was by achieving personal material success through all possible means. Cynicism and egoism were spread most widely among the youth, who lost any illusions about the system and its improvement, unlike the older, more idealistic generations. The youth were markedly different from the generation of the *shestidesyatniki* or the '60ers, who were intoxicated by destalinization and the thaw of the late 1950s and the 1960s and hoped for the creation of a "socialism with a human face." This explains why the new thaw of the 1980s did not excite the 20-year-old materialists, who were concerned only with personal material gains. The bulwark of early democratization from the 1980s was comprised of scientists, engineers, and other professionals in their forties and fifties, who resided primarily in the large industrial centers.

Noticeably more democratized are the "children of perestroika"—the generation 14–15 years old or even younger that grew up after 1985. The five-year period of democratization has created a cohort of young democrats. This age group finishing high school after 1991 is composed of the children of early and wild capitalism—capitalism of the street trade, of the mushrooming private enterprises, capitalism of the "quick ruble" and "quick buck" schemes, capitalism of the TV-advertised, 18-year-old millionaires, and capitalism responsible for the uncontrollable growth of crime.

The "roaring twenties" have begun in Russia, and what will become of the current 20-year-olds can only be guessed at. This group may become another "lost generation." At any rate, their lack of humanitarian concerns does not inspire confidence.

Meanwhile, among other social entities, the younger age group offers the most enthusiastic support for the formation of a market economy and for the radical changes in general. Evidence of this can be seen, for example, in table 4.5, where answers to two issues are examined: the need of a dictatorship to resolve crisis, and party support of different political orientations.

The greatest portion of the political continuum, the center, is comprised of a politically nonstructured mass of people, devoid of any clear-cut political orientation. They are exasperated by crisis and impoverishment. They do not trust anyone in power and are equally ready to lean either to the left or to the right. Alienation, disbelief, and anomie are typical responses from them, as they are from the majority of the population. Having lost Marx, they have not yet found Christ. A Magna Carta or a Bill of Rights has not yet been written for their use. The success of further democratic reform depends to a great extent on the behavior of this middle mass of people. The ability to influence the volatile and contradictory moods of this massive group is the key to the success of those politicians now in power or of those who, hopeful to follow, await their turn.

Quite indicative in this regard were elections to the parliament in December 1993 and particularly to its lower chamber, the State Duma; this was the first truly democratic election in Russia on a multiparty basis. According to the polls, one month before the election 29 percent of the voters did not know what party they would vote for. Answering the question about their interest in politics, 26 percent said that they have no interest whatsoever in politics, and another 34 percent stated that politics interests them only slightly.[32]

Among the political parties that took part in the campaign and were officially registered, the greatest amount of support was given to the governmental bloc, "Russia's Choice;" 16 percent of potential voters said one month before the election that they would vote for it. The second place, with 8% of potential voters, was occupied by the bloc headed by Grigory Yavlinsky, a young reform economist, who proposed an alternative program of economic reforms. Then followed the parties headed by Sobchak and by Shakhray, each with 4–5 percent of the voters. Finally, the Democratic party of Travkin, and Zhirinovsky's Liberal Democratic party of fascist or national socialist orientation, had support of less than 4 percent of the voters a piece.[33]

Not surprisingly, the people knew very little about the new parties, their programs, or even their general goals. This reaction could be predicted from what was said above about the public's low interest in politics and their general feeling of alienation. The whole campaign was essentially a competition of personalities, party leaders as seen on the TV screen. And many voters reported quite frankly in the polls that they support one or another party because they felt a "confidence in its leaders." Thirty-nine percent of the voters in an October poll responded as such. Another 15 percent cited the following as the chief reason for their party choice: "[the party] has the real power and can change the situation in the country." Only 13 percent said that they "knew the program of the party well and that it was close to [their] views." And another 11 percent made their choice "because this party or its leaders did not soil their reputation"; they did not compromise themselves on any grounds. The remaining number had not yet made up their minds.[34]

A week before the election the situation changed substantially; the publication of poll results had been banned ten days before the election. First place was still held by "Russia's Choice" (15 percent of potential voters), but second and the third places were divided by Yavlinsky and Zhirinovsky's parties—9 percent each. Finally, something very important, 21 percent had not made their choice yet.[35]

Election day results surprised everyone: Zhirinovsky's Liberal Democratic party came in first with 24 percent of the votes, followed by "Russia's Choice" with 14 percent of the votes. The communists took third place with 11 percent of the votes. Yavlinskiy bloc got only 8 percent.

As the first poll a week after the election has shown, 23 percent of the voters selected their political party during the last week of the election campaign, and 11 percent made up their minds on the day of the election.[36]

The "Zhirinovsky phenomenon" has already been described in a score of articles and books. It can be interpreted as the public's mass dissatisfaction with the disastrous reforms of the Yeltsin-Gaidar government. It is also seen as a condition receptive to the support of fascism in the country whose position is similar to Germany in the 1920s and the 1930s.

There is strong evidence for both of these explanations. In the fall of 1993 the level of public discontent with the government and its reforms had reached a menacing level. Forty-eight percent had revealed in a poll after the election that they selected a party because "I don't like the present leadership of the country and this way I wanted to show my attitude about the situation." Sixty-six percent mentioned that "in reality no party is the best and I have voted for this party because it is not as bad as the others."[37]

In their search for a "new face" and for a leader not linked to present or past governments, the population had selected a demagogue who promised to solve all problems at once as soon as his party took power. His actual political views did not matter much to the politically unsophisticated population.

Public support of Zhirinovsky's fascist pronouncements should be viewed in that sense—that having parted with communism, the Russian people had not acquired any other ideology. And it did not make much difference to them which party to support as long as its leader promised to solve the most painful problems of the country: the loss of Russia's greatness, the rising tide of crime and criminal behavior, the rising costs of the once inexpensive vodka, and a lack of confidence in the future. And above all if any party leader speaks and looks like a true and confident leader while at the same time remaining "one of us," he will earn the people's vote, as Zhirinovsky has.

It would be wrong to believe that in a country that had lost twenty-seven million people in a war against fascism, there appeared, out of nowhere, followers of fascism that represented 24 percent of the population. The results of the election in December 1993 have proven the thesis developed in this chapter: as a consequence of the breakdown of the political and ideological totalitarian system, the majority of the population were revealed to be deprived of any coherent system of political views. And—what may be even worse—they lacked most of the moral standards and values which could help them, in the absence of political landmarks, to steer a proper course—values to help them tell an effective humane leader from a political adventurer or a disguised fascist.

5

From Socialism to a Wild West Capitalism

In the mid-1980s on the eve of reform, there were no signs in mass public opinion that in just a few years the country would be converting to capitalism. The public's dissatisfaction with all material aspects of life was not spilling over into ideology, and their criticism was aimed mainly at traditional Russian-Soviet sins: the haphazard ways of running the economy, a pervasive laziness or indifference among the people, and systematic stealing by officials.

What concerned people most were the low standard of living and perpetual economic problems, which included constant shortages of food, especially in provinces away from Moscow; shortages of consumer goods; and the high price of many durable goods. Even though many families were barely making ends meet, huge personal savings were accumulated in the 1970s and the 1980s—in savings banks and in money-boxes—and these funds affected the consumer market, aggravating deficits and provoking speculation. A privileged group was created as a by-product of all this, the people of trade.

A special consumer culture of deficits and privileges was created during the Soviet era, when instead of using the common word "to buy," the public substituted its Soviet equivalent—"to obtain," i.e., to get on the black market or under the counter in a state shop, with the help of friendly tradesfolk or highly positioned persons. "Obtaining" was the only alternative to the endless hunt for a needed article; it was the only alternative to standing in lines.

In a somewhat better or different position were the Moscovites and the Leningraders whose main concern was to save money to pay for this or that "deficit"—especially prestigious foreign goods suddenly appearing in the stores. A universal Russian net bag *avoska,* from the word "perhaps," was quite handy for those occasions; it could be stored in one's pocket and unfolded if shopping proved propitious.

Streams of people were roaming the country, transporting meat, sausages, milk products, and fruits from the major centers to the provinces. Not that people were going hungry; rather, the diet of many was not nutritionally balanced. It was heavy on carbohydrates and lacked vitamins, and this combination contributed to a lower life expectancy and a rise in the child mortality rates, among other things.

Besides these problems of sustenance, the people were constantly concerned with the need to purchase other consumer goods. For some it was decent or modern clothing; for others, it was a refrigerator, a TV set, a stereo system, or furniture—an attempt to "keep up with the Joneses." The public's access to durable goods has undoubtedly grown since the 1960s; TV sets were practically in every family, but demand still grew. Television and travel beyond the Iron Curtain, at least to the other socialist countries of Eastern Europe, have created the consumption standards for this new group of consumers—the big city youth whose tastes approximated those of Eastern Europe and the rest of the world. But these standards also created feelings of inferiority within many youths of this group.

In the 1960s and 1970s, most people did not live in physical poverty. The Soviet socialism provided most people a minimal but guaranteed level of consumption, poor by Western standards but it did not leave citizens destitute. Also various social benefits were provided at that consumption level: free housing, medical care, and education, including a university education. The quality of these services was often criticized as low by world standards, but most of the public was not familiar with the standards outside Russia.

When Russians of the 1990s reminisce about this period of Soviet history, the quality they remember most from their lives is stability. A whole style of life, from standards of conduct to official regulations, did not change for decades. The rules of the game, however onerous, were known to everyone and did not change. Everyone knew what was allowed and what was not.

For example, if someone planned that in two years his monthly salary would rise by 50 rubles, he could confidently save money for a refrigerator, knowing that its price would remain the same. The purchaser might have to search many stores or wait in line, but at least he could expect to pay the same price.

Most of the public could accept this stable and modest level of consumption. "We were not rich, but we lived in humble sufficiency, and safely," recalled many from the departed epoch of 1980s' socialism. In one of the 1993 polls, people were asked, "In what period of time would they prefer to live, if they had a choice?" The largest group, 26 percent, chose the Brezhnev era; 15 percent selected the present; 13 percent, the remote future; 8 percent, the period of Andropov; 7 percent, before the Revolution; 5 percent, in remote past; 3 percent, at the time of Stalin; 2 percent, in Khrushchev's time; and less than 1 percent, during Gorbachev's era. Nineteen percent had no preference.[1]

It is obvious that the low consumption demands were created by the ruling ideology. Decades of communist propaganda, formal education, and the influence of mass culture had established a life style and a set of cultural expectations, which negated and condemned possessions, consumerism, and the cult of accumulation. Fighting the influence of individual freedoms in society, the system was also trying to limit the spread of material needs within the personality, which tended to promote the individual at the expense of the group. The ideal for this culture, therefore, was an ascetic "communist-idealist" who refused personal comforts for the good of the people and for class interests. An outward symbol of this type was the paramilitary uniform worn by the party bosses of all ranks until the 1950s. This style of uniform was not literally picked up by the masses, but its simplicity and modesty were widely emulated. This idea of eradicating the outward differences among people was fully implemented in China where blue paramilitary suits for men and women alike became the national uniform for decades.

In the Soviet Union, particularly in Russia, the equitable distribution of life's necessities was never so successful, and when income would allow, people tried to secure material possessions, not only for personal comfort but also as symbols of prestige and success. Even homes in the provinces with a modest income during the 1950s and the 1960s often had a cupboard with china and cut class used on holidays, a Middle Asiatic carpet, and a dust and moth collector. Later a TV set became a necessity, and not infrequently a piano would become part of the furniture.

No matter how strongly the official propaganda criticized this practice, calling it a middle-class convention or a life-style unacceptable to a communist, the desire to decorate or bring comfort to one's life by looking as prosperous as your neighbors or friends was ineradicable.

This desire to improve materially grew substantially during the 1960s, when the asceticism from the first five-year plans and from the war years was gradually replaced with the slogan from the Khruschev era—"satisfaction of growing material and cultural needs of the Soviet people." This reversal of ideological doctrine was brought about by a change in official policy: it represented a movement from Stalin's complete isolation to a peaceful competition with capitalism. This change was fueled by the Soviet necessity to compete with the West not only in rocketry but also in living standards.

With a more open society this competition led to increases in consumer goods production. In the 1960s the public was more fashionably attired, and the supplies of consumer goods from the East European socialist countries were largely responsible for this change. Concurrently, the official doctrine was promoting the "regulation of needs" and using the communist customs for modesty, however contradictory it was to their principle, "satisfaction of growing needs." Khrushchev declared, for instance, that the Soviet Union would not follow the West in developing private automobile transport but instead would have the best public transportation system in the world. Public enthusiasm over the rapid construction of subways in major cities could not quell the dissatisfaction of many people who had to set aside their dream of private car ownership for many years.

If the official propaganda successfully managed to eradicate from the public mind a desire to become an owner of real or private property—a store, an auto repair shop, a factory, or some other property for production, which contradicted the socialist principle of state ownership of production sources—a desire to own some personal property persisted. Seven decades of the state limiting, banning, and condemning through its propaganda machines could not completely destroy the public's desire for a humble piece of land in the country or a vegetable garden or a small, privately owned house.

This growing materialism of the post-Stalinist era was far from reformist. Its consequences, criticism of the economy's mismanagement and the low standard of living, did not lead to a revision of socialism in the public mind, much less to a replacement of socialism with capitalism. For many citizens the examples to follow were found in the much more effective and affluent socialist countries of Eastern Europe. Some would even go as far as to mention the higher efficiency in the West. But the aims of even these people was always to achieve the abundant and superior goods and services of capitalism while retaining the social values of socialism—guaranteed employment by the state and free housing, medical services, and education.

On the wave of the post-Stalinist thaw of the late 1950s and into the 60s, some ideas began to develop about reforming the socialist economy. Arising first among the intelligentsia, they gradually spread to a broader public. Central to these ideas was the belief that the socialist economy is flawed through its excessive centralization and control from the center, with little independence or freedom given to the subordinate enterprises. Thus an expression was proposed, "cost-accounting," which is difficult to translate into a standard economic language. It referred to substantially more economic independence for the enterprises, which continued to operate as socialist, state-owned entities but retained some of their profit deriving from their productivity. This concept was expected to increase radically the people's incentives for raising labor productivity. It became a widely spread belief that this plan was the essence of Lenin's New Economic Policy from the 1920s, to which the country should return.

Similar plans to improve or perfect socialism continued to surface in the 1980s. Most of them were centered around proposals to partially decentralize the state planning of production and distribution so that the production of every spoon and nail need not be controlled from Moscow. Because most attempts at reform were opposed by powerful party and government bureaucracies and existed only on paper, economic efficiency continued to decline. The public's frustration increased as the empty rhetoric about reform increased.

The people's dissatisfaction with the condition of the economy and their standard of living was producing for the three decades from the 1960s through the 1980s a growing cynicism, a reduced worker efficiency, absenteeism, and the mass pilferage of state property.

Many people criticized the socialist economy with their feet; they tried to flee the country. The Jewish emigration to Israel and to the United States was growing; others were trying to leave for other "countries of capital." Within the Soviet Union itself a type of internal emigration was emerging: millions of people were in fact leaving the socialist sector by parasitizing off it. The trade personnel were living by speculation, reselling scarce consumer goods under the counter. Members of the "shadow economy" were illegally producing in secret shops various goods and selling them for profit, and from this activity a growing criminal world developed. Finally, millions of otherwise law-abiding citizens began stealing from socialist enterprises everything they could put their hands on.

Whatever constructive criticism the people had, it centered on the different ways to modify, modernize, or perfect socialism. And this was the economic consciousness with which the public approached the threshold of radical economic reform in the mid-1980s.

The Last Five-Year Plan of Socialism

As mentioned in chapter 2, reformers would try in the beginning to improve socialism without changing its principles: "tightening the nuts" of discipline, saving resources, speeding up production using command controls, targeting key branches of industry—machine manufacture and electronics. Economic methods were also used, i.e., modifying control over prices, wages, and taxes. Then the experiments with market strategies began.

Looking back at the period from 1985 (the beginning of perestroika) to 1992 (when drastic measures of reform were introduced), one can only marvel at the radical changes that took place in the country over seven short years—the great leaps forward and the efforts to turn back, as one team of reformers was replaced with another. Whatever the critics of reform on the left and on the right are saying now, the country has departed from socialism and is building some kind of capitalism. The outcome of all this is far from clear, but some conclusions are undeniable: the leap in seven years was enormous, and the mass consciousness was absolutely unprepared for it.

The public's lack of preparation for radical reform was in part due to the reformers: they were not explaining what was going on to the people. On the one hand, reform theoreticians could not conceive of how the products of reform would look, and therefore each new team had its own vision of the future. On the other hand, because of the continuing struggle for power between democrats and communists, most discussions about reform had to be camouflaged in the rhetoric of "improving" socialism, even though most economists surrounding Gorbachev and Yeltsin clearly understood that a market economy was being built and that this economy was a form of capitalism. But until 1992 most publications in the press were filled with jargon, like "socialism with market elements," "market socialism," and "regulated market."

Therefore, a popular slogan of the time—"more socialism, more democracy"—was not compatible with the new laws that were allowing some forms of private property or cooperatives or forms of free trade on the streets. Many discussions on the topic of reforms notwithstanding, the public still could not understand why the idea of socialist property (for the good of production) was not necessary. Nor could they understand how private property can be combined with socialism: how equality and social justice can be maintained if some people, e.g., cooperative members, might be getting much more for the same work than workers of the regular state enterprises. The public could not understand why working for a private owner of a store or repair shop ceased to be an exploitation—how can we even think of the possibility of unemployment in the nation after we liberated ourselves forever from this "pest of capitalism"?

Besides these theoretical questions asked by many people, much of the public has come to believe from the very beginning that nothing good will come of reform. Already in December 1990, a VCIOM poll has shown that when asked what the public associated market economy with, 54 percent replied "rise in prices," 34 percent said "differentiation into the rich and the poor," and another 23 percent mentioned "lowering the standard of living."[2] The complete picture of public expectations of the transition to market economy is shown in table 5.1. Subsequent events has supported these pessimistic expectations of the public.

Instead of preparing people for inevitable forthcoming hardships, the reform theoreticians were following the logic that transition to market, liberating initiative, and increasing material incentives for people, would lead to a growth in production. Competition would increase the quality of goods, and liberated prices would, on average, remain the same as before the reforms—unjustifiably high prices would go down and very low prices would rise.

The ambiguous, even contradictory statements of government ministers and economists made many people feel that the government itself does not fully understand in what direction they are moving the reforms. Answering the question whether "the leadership of the USSR has a well thought-out program for a solution to the economic crisis," 51 percent said that there was no such program; only 14 percent believed such a program existed, and 35 percent did not answer.[3]

Lulling promises notwithstanding, the people were anxious about the radical steps to move toward a market economy, and they hoped to delay this painful process as much as possible. In a 1990 poll only 19 percent insisted that the transition to the market should be done as quickly as possible, while 40 percent believed that "transition is necessary, but it should be performed gradually," and 16 percent said that transition to the market should not be made at all. Twenty-five percent did not have any specific point of view. The highest level of support for

Table 5.1

"What do you mainly associate market economy with?"

(in percentage)

Answer	USSR					Russia	Ukraine	Estonia
	Avg.	Under 24	Above 55	College	High School			
Rise in prices	54	57	51	45	54	55	54	35
Differentiation into rich and poor	34	31	36	34	31	36	27	35
Lowering the standard of living	23	12	30	19	19	26	25	13
Unemployment	22	22	21	20	23	22	28	16
Improving the economy	20	23	18	34	21	20	17	38
Raising the standard of living	19	19	16	20	20	17	19	24
Filling stores with consumer goods	16	21	14	19	18	18	16	19
Freedom of enterprise	14	18	8	26	16	14	10	37
Private property	14	20	12	20	15	14	11	23
Competition	12	15	6	17	13	11	13	40
Capitalism	5	7	5	5	5	4	4	3

Source: VCIOM Omnibus poll, Dec. 1990.

transition to market was shown by people with a college education, as has been the case until recently; 36 percent of them advocated speedy transition, 41 percent were for gradual reforms, and only 9 percent disapproved of transition at all.[4]

The public had experienced life in a semimarket economy, and in the fall of 1993, people were providing the following assessments about the speed of transition. Their general attitude about the market economy was still quite skeptical: 33 percent preferred the system "that is mostly based on the state planning and distribution," while 39 percent supported the system based on the "market relations and private property," with 28 percent having no opinion.[5] And apparently trying to end this intolerably painful stage, many preferred to accelerate the reforms and not to experience a gradual transition to the market. In October 1993 35 percent of the people believed that "reforms are going too slowly," another 11 percent said that reforms were proceeding at a proper pace, 39 percent thought that there were no reforms at all, and only 15 percent believed that the reforms were proceeding too quickly.[6]

When a question was asked in a more theoretical, descriptive manner (as in the poll from 1990), the reaction was more prosocialist: "would you support economic reform which would allow the most energetic and resourceful people to triple their incomes, while incomes of the rest would increase only by a few percentage points?" Thirty-five percent agreed with such a reform, while 65 percent disagreed.[7] With this question it is possible that people were intimidated by the triple increase in income. In general the socialist ideal of the equal distribution of pay was spread quite widely: it is better when everyone gets little; then no one stands out.

Typical also of the Russian mind is the belief that "it is better to have a modest but stable income and confidence in the future." This motto is probably the essence of the socialist attitude about work and income, and it is shared by about 40 percent of the population. In a 1992 poll 38 percent subscribed to this belief, while 28 percent were more market oriented and believed that "it is better to work hard and get a good income, even without special guarantees for the future." Finally, those people with a "full-market" mentality, 12 percent, preferred to "have their own business and run it at their own risk."[8] A year later, in the summer of 1993, a majority, 52 percent, preferred a "guaranteed, though not high income," while only 22 percent chose a "high income without guarantees for the future." Twenty-six percent found it difficult to answer.[9]

The Difficult Lot of Private Property in Russia

The attitude toward private property has been a pivotal problem in the transition to a market economy. If the population is not ready to transform state ownership of production into privately owned industrial plants, transportation systems, and land, and if enough people are not ready to take into possession such property and become entrepreneurs, a market economy does not have much of a chance for immediate success. Here public beliefs were quite confused and overloaded with stereotypes from communist propaganda; these beliefs depend to a great extent on the nation's economic condition.

One area of confusion was the official theory about the differences between individual and private property and how the former transforms into the latter when it begins to bring in profit not earned with one's personal labor.

The whole history of Soviet power is the history of the state's struggle of the most ugly kind with private property and "unearned income." In the 1930s it included "dispossession of the kulaks" in the villages and then limitations on the "subsidiary household plots of collective farmers," i.e., the right for peasants to have a cow or other stock. In the cities this "struggle" took the form of persecution. All too common was the baiting of a *chastnik*, a small businessman or entrepreneur, the private tailor, the street trader, or the private citizen who leases his apartment or a room from it or who gives someone a lift in his car for money—any form of work for one's personal gain and not for the benefit of the entire society.

One of the first surveys of public attitudes about property was conducted in November 1989 during discussion of the law on property in the USSR Supreme Soviet.[10] Many deputies claimed that their constituencies categorically rejected on principle any proposal permitting the acquisition of private property in industry or agriculture. The survey showed a rather diverse set of views with a substantial level of support for private property in different forms, although with various limitations. The leadership of the Supreme Soviet was displeased with the poll results; it contradicted their claims, and they tried to hide the results from the deputies. A scandal erupted, resulting in Parliament requesting VCIOM to conduct a similar survey with a larger sample. The survey was carried out a month later, and its results were similar; they proved instrumental in passing the law on property, a law more liberal and more congruent to the public views.[11]

The controversial mass views on private property are reflected in

Table 5.2
"Can the following be called private property?"
(in percentage)

Answer	Yes	No	No Answer
A house, a car, a summer cottage (dacha), savings belonging to a person.	67	26	7
Enterprises belonging to private persons, where only they and their family members work.	63	18	19
Enterprises belonging to private persons (plants, stores, repair shops, etc.) with hired workers.	52	28	20
Property of cooperatives.	30	40	30
Enterprises bought from the state by their workers' collectives.	34	36	30

Source: N. P. Popov and S. Shpilko, "Attitudes about Property," VCIOM report, Jan. 1990.

the results of a January 1990 survey concerning attitudes about different forms of property, specifically in answer to the question "what can be called private property?" (See table 5.2.)

The majority associated private property with what was identified by official propaganda as individual property. When the means of production using hired labor was involved, half of those polled did not attribute them to private property at all or could not offer any opinion.

These vague notions of what private property is, mixed with stereotypes about what is and is not permissible by socialist standards, continues to influence the public's attitudes toward the various new forms of property and indeed toward the entire process of privatization or the denationalization of industry.

These views can be illustrated in the public's attitudes toward the different property arrangements within industry—from using property leased from the state by working collectives to participating in fully private ownership of enterprises, as shown in table 5.3.

The collective forms of property ownership obviously enjoy much greater support than purely private ownership. But foreign firms, apparently privately owned, are respected more than domestic ones for their expected higher efficiency and consequent usefulness to the country. Another conclusion: small private shops are quite welcome; the large ones should not be allowed. Cooperatives received the high-

Table 5.3
"What is your attitude to the following forms of ownership of enterprises?"
(in percentage)

Answer	Positive	Indifferent	Negative	Difficult to Answer
Enterprises leased by working collectives from the state	70	8	7	15
Enterprises owned by working collectives	70	9	5	16
Joint ventures owned by the state and foreign firms	69	5	12	14
Enterprises created from the funds of stock holders	45	12	15	28
Enterprises owned by foreign companies	36	7	36	21
Cooperatives	30	12	42	16
Enterprises belonging to private individuals	27	10	40	23

Source: N. P. Popov and S. Shpilko, "Attitudes about Property," VCIOM report, Jan. 1990.

est negative ratings in the polls, 42 percent. The reason is simple: this early form of nongovernmental property was the first to be permitted under the reform laws. Their activities were clearly visible and so were their higher profits, especially when compared with profits from the state enterprises. In the public's mind this was an unjustly earned profit, and co-ops became for a few years a symbol of greedy profiteering within the emerging business class.

The size of enterprises also significantly influences or affects the public's attitudes about ownership. Small repair shops, dressmaker shops, or stores were regarded by 28 percent as necessary, and 45 percent believed that "they can be allowed," while only 6 percent thought that large plants and factories should be privately owned and 17 percent believed that such ownership might be allowed.[12]

The willingness to support private ownership of commercial enterprises varies with the commercial area of activity or service (see table

Table 5.4
"In what activities is it necessary (or allowable or inadmissible) to set up privately owned businesses?"
(in percentage)

Answer	Necessary	Allowable	Inadmissible	Difficult to Answer
Agricultural Produce	38	38	12	12
Light Industry	19	40	22	20
School Education	16	33	33	18
Health Care	16	32	36	16
Automobile Production	9	19	45	27
Machine Building	6	16	48	30
Defense Industry	4	5	67	24

Source: N. P. Popov and S. Shpilko, "Attitudes about Property," VCIOM report, Jan. 1990.

5.4). Most of the public was prepared to allow privatization in the food processing and other light industries, even at the beginning of reform (which cannot be said about heavy industries). The public also supported development of private business in traditionally socialized areas like health care and education. The public had grown increasingly more discontent with the quality of these services over the last decades, and many people, putting their principles aside, were eager to pay for better medical treatment and education for their children.

The public attitudes about the use of hired labor at private enterprises are very important to understanding the public's economic beliefs at the beginning of reform. The solution to this problem, i.e., whether this "exploitation of man by man" should be allowed, will be decisive in the transition from socialism to capitalism for the public.

A relative majority therefore, 42 percent, considered use of hired labor at private enterprises inadmissible, while 38 percent thought it was at least possible. Of the latter group, 13 percent would approve of any number hired by a private owner; another 13 percent, "many workers;" and 12 percent, "just a few, not more than ten people."[13] Obviously those negative attitudes about "exploitation" held by 42 percent —no hired labor at private enterprises—actually meant rather low support for the very idea of private property and market reform, even though the majority expressed support in principle. But such is the

Table 5.5
Principal Results of the National Appearance of Private Property
(in percentage)

Result	
Return of the feeling of true ownership	51
Growth of material differentiation	36
Disappearance of consumer goods shortages	26
General improvement of economic conditions	25
Beginning of exploitation of man by man	17
Rejection of socialist achievements	10

Source: N. P. Popov and S. Shpilko, "Attitudes about Property," VCIOM report, Jan. 1990.

contradictory nature of the Russian mass consciousness. This general or middle-of-the-road support is illustrated, for example, in the opinions of 47 percent, who thought that the arrival or "appearance of these enterprises owned by private persons would better the economic situation in the country." Only 15 percent believed the opposite.[14]

This contradictory attitude toward private property, embracing both the positive and the negative sides, is reflected in the answer to the question "what would be the principle results of the appearance of private property in our country?" (See table 5.5.)

If the various assessments about the public's private property attitudes are compared and analyzed at the onset of radical economic reform, the following conclusions can be drawn. The first group, comprising 12 percent of the population, included consistent supporters of private property who approved of the existence of large private enterprises with a substantial number of hired workers. The second group, 23 percent of the population, were supporters of private property but only of small businesses with a limited number of hired workers. The third group, 38 percent, would permit only individual or family businesses on the basis of some private property, and without hired help. And finally, 14 percent were in principle against any form of private property. Thirteen percent had no opinion on these issues.[15]

Following three years of private property growth—through spontaneous emergence of businesses and through state programs to privatize enterprises in commercial trade, in the services, and in manufacturing—the public expressed these attitudes about private property in the summer of 1993. About 5 percent reported that they have started their own business or farm. Thirty percent stated that they would like to start up or buy their own business, and 53 percent answered that they did not wish to own their own business. Another 13% did not reply.[16]

Kolkhozes or Private Farmers?

During these critical years of unfolding economic reform, a most acute discussion ensued: what kind of agricultural reformation should be effected and who should own the land? The need for agrarian reform was obvious to anyone. Ignoring the famines of the 1920s and 1930s (resulting from the Bolsheviks robbing the peasants), the record shows that the collective and state farms could not provide enough produce to feed the country during the Soviet era. There constantly were shortages of food or, if stock levels were adequate, prices were too high for most people. The inefficiency of socialist agriculture had become notorious. Kolkhozes and sovkhozes were subjects of continued criticism. But in the 1960s and the 1970s, this criticism and subsequent demand for reform focused on giving more independence to kolkhozes and ending the petty tutelage over them by local party chiefs and other authorities.

In the early 1980s it was no longer a secret that those kolkhozniks with tiny household plots were raising as many vegetables for sale as the whole socialist sector in agriculture. Their efforts demonstrated the miracles of efficiency because they were working for their own profit and not for the state. By the time of reform, discussion of this subject in the press and within the public had created a fertile soil for the increasing acceptance of this type of agriculture, which allowed family farming with the ownership of land in one form or another.

This idea was gaining more and more support, especially among city dwellers who, in principle, embraced the idea throughout their general discussions of democratization. The peasants, however, viewed all innovations affecting them with great suspicion.

For the peasants, innovation threatened to destroy a habitual way of life, a life with a significantly low but stable income, little responsibility or risk, and low labor intensity—in other words, with every characteristic of the socialist economy. Development of individual farming meant competition to many kolkhozniks, and they feared that private farmers would produce cheaper goods and push them out of the market. Finally, for many peasants the very idea that someone next door could earn more money, especially by hard work, evoked envy and dislike.

At the beginning of reform in the late 1980s, these feelings about competitive production were combined with the general ideological stereotypes surrounding the concept of property. Private ownership of land, which should belong to the whole society according to Marxist theory, is inadmissible for many traditionalists from an ideological or philosophical standpoint. Here, the same logic is used as was applied to the case of industrial property: permitted are subsidiary household property—a small private plot, a personal vegetable garden, an orchard, or some cattle—even though they are privately owned like the small shop or store in town. But privately owned large lots of land with large-scale production were inappropriate, as were large industrial plants in private hands.

Attitudes toward land use and property in agriculture were probed in the survey of November 1989, when a draft of the law on property was discussed in the Supreme Soviet. The public preference for various types of farming is revealed in the data of table 5.6.

Individual farming was supported by 35 percent of the specialists; 29 percent of the blue-collar workers; 39 percent of the urban population; and 33 percent of the villagers—more of them were for the continuation of kolkhozes and sovkhozes.[17]

Another important issue, which still persists, is the mechanism by which the land should be turned over to private ownership; what legal and financial arrangements should be made. As table 5.7 shows, the respondents supporting private property on the land have separated into two roughly equal groups: those (40 percent) who believe the land should be given to farmers without the right to resell it later and those (36 percent) who think that possession of the land should include the right to resale.[18]

A year later, in February 1991, a survey conducted on the draft of the new Russian Constitution, which included land reform, showed an increase (to 40 percent) in the number of supporters who favor relinquishing the land to private ownership without any limitations, including resale, with 52 percent favoring land rights transfer with some limitations.[19]

These limitations were of two types. One limitation dealt with the size of the plot. One-third believed that it should not exceed 15 hectares or 37 acres, while two-thirds were prepared to support privatization of larger lots.

The second limitation concerned to whom the land should be

Table 5.6
Preferred Forms of Property and Land Use
(in percentage)

Preferred Forms	
Farms belonging to private owners	34
Farmers leasing land	26
Kolkhozes	19
Sovkhozes (state farms)	16
New agricultural cooperatives (different from kolkhozes)	12
Difficult to answer	14

Source: N. P. Popov and S. Shpilko, "Attitudes Toward the Law on Property," VCIOM report, Dec. 1989.
Note: Sum exceeds 100% because respondents could choose more than one answer.

Table 5.7
"Should the land be turned over to individual owners and in what form?"
(in percentage)

Answer	Rural Dwellers	Urban Dwellers
The land should not be turned over to individual owners.	5	7
The land should be leased for pay, without the right to sell it to other people.	15	17
The land should be given free of charge, but without the right to sell it.	40	36
The land should be turned over to people free, with the right to sell it to others.	14	9
The state should sell the land to whomever wants to own it, with the right to resell it.	21	6
Do not know or question not answered.	5	6

Source: L. A. Khakhulina, "Attitudes about Property on Land," VCIOM report, Jan. 1990.

sold, if the private owner desires to resell it. There was popular interest that the land should only be resold to the state so that the government could control the process of land redistribution. This idea got support of 39 percent. Twenty-eight percent believed that new private owners should have the right to resell the land to anyone.[20] This results in two-thirds of the public supporting the idea of buying and selling privately owned land. The trend continued into 1992 and 1993 and represents a significant change since the beginning of discussions about land reform law four years ago.

The reluctance of peasants to support land privatization has also slackened somewhat, as the data of the 1991 and 1992 surveys show in table 5.8, although the majority of peasants still disapproved of private ownership of large pieces of land: 33 percent for it and 52 percent against it.[21] The Russians are not yet ready for large, privately owned pieces of land.

A sudden change (within one year) in peasants' predispositions toward the forms of land property—from disapproval to approval by the majority—should not be accepted at face value. Their new support for private property is theoretical to a certain degree. Following the general liberal-democratic mood of the time, many of them began to think that the Soviet kolkhoz-sovkhoz agricultural system reached the limit of its resources, and this belief became prevalent in the general public in 1992. But at the practical level many peasants believed that private farmers could not supply the whole country with enough produce, and therefore kolkhozes and sovkhozes should also remain. Consequently, only about 10 percent of them considered becoming private farmers. Many were young men with a secondary professional education who worked as professionals on collective or state farms. This rather limited group of younger and better-educated farmers is so far the basis for developing private farming.

Besides the older, less educated farmers who are not going to go into private farming, many others have been frightened off because they don't trust the new laws allowing private property and private farming, and they are wary of the despotism of local government authorities and the management of kolkhozes and sovkhozes.

Also contrary to the popular notion that peasants, with their subsidiary plots of land and their own house, traditionally are proprietors to much greater extent than townspeople and thus ready to extend their property, the peasants' enthusiasm to privatize is actually limited. Their reluctance is based on typically Soviet socialist concerns—fear of losing small but guaranteed incomes from their kolkhoz without any

Table 5.8
"Do you approve or disapprove of turning over the land to private owners with the right of resale or inheritance?"
(in percentage)

Answer	1991	1992
Yes	35	52
No	47	34
Do not know or question not answered	18	14

Source: VCIOM rural surveys; May 1991, July 1992.

guarantee of success in private business, and fear of the envy and animosity engendered in their neighbors, should their income grow. Unlike the rest of the world where shame was connected with poverty, these people were afraid to earn more.

Reliance on the State or on One's Own Strength

Success of the reforms depends to a great degree on development of initiative and an entrepreneurial spirit, and that in turn is closely connected to attitudes of self-reliance on one hand or the feeling of dependency or reliance on the state on the other. The public's reaction about this is quite mixed and these views represent a combination of traditional beliefs cultivated by the Soviet socialist systems for decades (total tutelage of the state over the lives of the people) mixed with attitudes created by an economic reality based on personal experience during the first years of radical reforms.

The correlation between feelings of self-reliance and dependence on the state was measured from the beginning of reform. In a joint 1989 Soviet-American survey of the USSR population, 42 percent expressed the opinion that "the state should be responsible for people's successes and well-being" while a somewhat bigger number, 50 percent, believed that the "people should take care of themselves, make their own decisions, and take whatever measures for success." Eight percent did not have an answer.[22]

Another issue related to this problem was whether poor people should be blamed for their plight. Forty-two percent believed that "it is these people's fault," and almost an equal number felt that the "causes of personal poverty are in circumstances outside their control." Eleven percent had no answer.

Finally, a third issue approached the problem of self-reliance from the perspective of equality of income. Material equality was claimed to be an important goal of socialist development, and income differentiating was supposed to be minimal. In the survey 81 percent had the view that "the state should allow everyone to earn as much as one can," while only 15 percent were supporting the equal distribution principle —"the state should in every way try to minimize differences in people's incomes and standard of living."

Thus, more than 80 percent supported the entrepreneurial efforts of people and their desire to earn more. But at the same time one-half of the population believed that the reasons for poverty were external, and more than 40 percent thought that the state should be responsible for the people's well-being. In other words, people do not quite understand the nature of economic risk; they are ready to display initiative and other entrepreneurial qualities but in times of adversity still prefer to rely on the support of the state. On the one hand they are ready to support people who try to earn more, but on the other when such people do appear, they demand that the state either raise the income of the rest or curtail the income of the more fortunate ones.

Attitudes from the younger and better educated strata of society are filled with more support for individual initiative and independence, as compared with older people (table 5.9) and those with lower education levels.

In general, attitude differences concerning this problem are not great among the various social groups. The differences are more noticeable among geographical areas or regions of the then Soviet Union (see table 5.10). The people of Kazakhstan seemed to be more oriented toward self-reliance, while the population of Ukraine and Georgia showed more dependence on the state. More controversial were the responses of the people from Uzbekistan, Russia, and Estonia.

These views are fluctuating greatly now, depending on rapid changes in the economic situation and on the new experiences people are acquiring every day in a market-oriented environment. But there is still a widespread belief both in Russia and in the other republics of the former Soviet Union that the responsibility for the people's well being resides with the state. This is especially true in time of crisis when the people demand social protection.

The character and level of these demands show up quite clearly in the 1991 survey on the draft of the new Constitution of the Russian

Table 5.9
Comparison of Attitudes about Self-Reliance vs. Government Support by Age Group
(in percentage)

Attitude	Below 25	25–29	30–59	60 and Over
The state should be responsible for the welfare of people	41	46	47	50
People should take care of themselves	50	49	43	41

Source: B. Grushin, N. Popov, A. Finifter, G. Gerbner, and E. Mickiewicz, "Television and Society," Soviet-American Study of Public Opinion, report, Mar. 1991.

Federation, where substantial changes in the Constitution were proposed in state social security guarantees, specifically, in health care, housing, and education.[23] The philosophy behind these changes was that, in line with the development of market relations, there should be provisions both that services be supplied by the state *and* that individuals be allowed to pay for their own services, if they wish.

The survey has demonstrated that, contrary to the assessments of the political groups and the press, the Russian population is already using paid services quite extensively, is ready to support both socialized and private or paid social services, and would approve incorporating both positions into the new Constitution. For instance, in the area of medical care, 38 percent felt it necessary to put in the Constitution "the right of citizens to paid medical services." Thirty-seven percent disagreed.

There are more supporters of paid medicine among the youth than among the older generations. Prosperous people, of course, supported it more enthusiastically but even among the low income groups the levels of support and disapproval are almost equal, 45 and 47 percents respectively. Among occupational groups, the lowest level of support for paid health care was among the peasants, 45 percent for and 59 percent against. The highest support came from skilled workers; 61 percent for it and 35 percent against it.[24]

It may sound strange that people are demanding the right to pay for something when they would otherwise get it free, but this observation reflects a fundamental change in the public's outlook.

People do not believe that, if they keep demanding radical im-

Table 5.10

Differences of Opinion by Geographical Areas

(in percentage)

Opinion	Russia	Ukraine	Byelorussia	Kazakhstan	Uzbekistan	Estonia	Georgia
The state should be responsible for the welfare of people.	45	53	40	33	46	42	74
People should take care of themselves.	47	35	49	55	49	46	25
Poverty is the fault of the poor.	40	30	44	47	61	25	25
Causes of poverty are outside the person's control.	49	58	43	36	32	53	71
The state should allow everyone to earn as much as one can.	86	87	79	81	66	90	95
The state should try in every way to minimize differences in people's income and standard of living.	10	9	19	13	28	7	4

Source: B. Grushin, N. Popov, A. Finifter, G. Gerbner, and E. Mickiewicz, "Television and Society," Soviet-American Study of Public Opinion, report, Mar. 1991.

provement from the generally acknowledged substandard state-owned health services, they will achieve the needed results; the public simply does not trust the state any longer. So they would rather pay for these services (which they were already doing at the time of the survey) than stand in long lines to get substandard treatment at state clinics and hospitals. This change also reflects their new taste of freedom, the freedom of choice: the ability to decide for themselves whether they are going to receive a guaranteed social service of uncertain quality or to seek something better. Finally, this signifies a departure from the principle of equality; people clearly want some things of better quality for themselves and medical care is one of those services.

One-third of the population supports these new approaches, another third still supports traditional socialized health care, and the rest have no particular preference. Medical insurance, as an alternative to services paid for out of pocket, is just beginning to be discussed.

Similar attitudes were expressed toward private and paid school education. Fifty-one percent said that "both free and paid school education should be allowed" and that these rights should be an integral part of the Constitution. Forty-three percent supported the traditional approach of free, state-run education, and 6 percent had no opinion.[25] The attitudes from the various sociodemographic groups about this issue are parallel to their beliefs about paid medical services. Generally speaking, there is a growing desire among people to provide the legal foundation necessary to get the kind of services they can afford.

A comparable reaction could be seen with the housing issue. Traditionally, the government built apartment houses and distributed them free to the public with a symbolically low rent. Most people seemed satisfied with this arrangement, and the only complaint concerned long waiting lists. The survey has shown some substantial changes in attitudes about the housing problem—and in ways for solving the problem (see table 5.11).

The largest support was shown for the state's substantial role in providing housing for the public but with the possibility, for those who could afford it, to buy an apartment and improve the quality of this public service. About one-quarter supported the traditional Soviet position—specifically, free housing provided by the state with some cooperative construction. And the lowest level of support, 13 percent, has embraced the idea, which is becoming the state policy now, of drastic cuts in the state financing of public housing and the provision of free housing only to the poorest population groups. At a time of deep economic crisis and huge budget deficit, this position is becoming the current state policy.

Table 5.11

"What kind of housing provisions should be recorded in Russian law?"

(in percentage)

Type of Housing	
Provision only for state-owned apartments and for cooperative apartments with state subsidy.	26
Provision for state apartments with size limitations and permission to buy bigger apartments through private, cooperative construction.	37
Provision for state apartments only to the needy and private or cooperative construction to the rest of people.	13
Only private or cooperative construction for everybody.	3
Do not know or question not answered.	21

Source: N. Popov and R. Volkova, "The New Constitution of the Russian Federation and Public Opinion," VCIOM report, Mar. 1991.

An Unheard-of Menace: Unemployment

Even with the Russian public now quite familiar with numerous material problems—housing shortages and crowded living condition in communal apartments, high prices and shortages of consumer goods, often difficult manual work in industry and agriculture—at least one problem was unknown to the current generations, unemployment. From a public point of view (stimulated by the decades of propaganda), work made compulsory by law with the guaranteed right to a job was the greatest social achievement of socialism. The reality, however, was that full employment was artificially maintained at the expense of low productivity.

The absence of, the search for, and the loss of work were all considered features of capitalism and simply did not exist within the socialist reality. Accordingly, even the remote threat of unemployment was not considered seriously by the public. Even when economists and the press at the time of the Gorbechev-Ryzhkov government in 1988–90 began to discuss the possibility of unemployment in a transitory period to market economy, the majority of the public did not take it seriously. From the end of the 1980s until 1993, the public puts unemployment in fifth place among a list of problems that bothered them most—after high prices, shortages of goods, general chaos, lawlessness and crime.

And until recently the state was considered the main guarantor against unemployment.

Even if the public was expecting a decline in the state's willingness to provide other benefits, it was in the area of employment that the majority still believed in the state's obligation to provide people with jobs. This response is explained partially by the deep socialist orientations of many citizens—the state's responsibility to organize everything. Some people also believed that because most enterprises were still run by the state (i.e., not private), the state can still regulate the number of people employed within this huge governmental sector of the economy.

Under pressure from the lobby of the state-owned industrial enterprises, a certain role in calming the public was played by the state, which has delayed passage of the bankruptcy law for state enterprises. The resulting continuation of subsidies to unprofitable enterprises was restraining any increase in mass unemployment in 1991–93, and this practice led people to believe that the alleged unemployment was an improbability and not very menacing.

Attitudes about the state's role to provide people with jobs during the transition to a market economy were revealed in the survey of 1991 (see table 5.12).

Nine out of ten people polled believed that, even with the development of nongovernmental enterprises and market relations, the state is obligated to provide people with jobs. Moreover, the majority believed that employment should be provided in the same occupation and qualification as the previous position. And besides 92 percent believed that the state "should provide people who lost jobs with vocational training, so that they could get a job in a new profession." Ninety-two percent also thought that the state should provide people who lose jobs with unemployment compensation.[26]

In the spring of 1993, the level of joblessness had reached 1 percent of labor force for the first time in a half-century, after a number of years of alarming forecasts by economists about unemployment. It remained at this point for the rest of the year. Surveys from the summer of 1993 have shown that 12 percent of working people felt it very likely they might lose their job, 25 percent believed that such a possibility existed, and 51 percent considered it improbable.

Asked about the situation at their own enterprises, almost half (46 percent) reported that there was the threat of "considerable cuts in the number of employed," with 41 percent saying that no such threat existed at their enterprises.[27]

Table 5.12

"What should be the role of the state in employment?"

(in percentage)

Answer	
The state should provide everyone with a job in accordance with one's education and occupation.	56
The state should provide people who lost jobs with any kind of job.	32
The state should not deal with the problems of employment. This is their own concern.	5
Do not know or question not answered.	7

Source: N. Popov and R. Volkova, "The New Constitution of the Russian Federation and Public Opinion," VCIOM report, Mar. 1991.

At the same time there are signs that the presence of unemployment is becoming a habitual feature of the society, and the unemployed have evolved from their position of "exotic sect" into a regular, normal group in the society with nothing to be ashamed of.

The population in general, and working people in particular, began to relax their demands that the state provide jobs for the unemployed "in accordance with one's education and occupation" and guarantee at least some jobs. There were also growing feelings that some of the unemployed were making excessive demands on employment offices and rejecting good job offers, preferring compensation to work. The growth of such sentiments was revealed in our survey of the unemployed in the summer of 1993, in which one-third of those polled reported knowing of such an attitude, which had been reported to them by working people.[28]

Even though the level of unemployment is still relatively low, the very existence of a sizable number of people looking for jobs, sometimes any job, combined with a growing fear about losing one's job, creates stress in people's lives and can lead to strained relations at work and growing social tension in the society. The way people described the changing relations at work is revealed in an April 1993 survey (see table 5.13).

Tension between people who fear losing their jobs is not unique to Russia; it is characteristic of other countries in crisis as well. But in Russia with its rather stable etatist beliefs within the population, the state, the government, and the leaders of economic reform are held accountable for this additional calamity, and they are supposed to pro-

Table 5.13
"How has the fear of losing a job influenced the behavior of the people of your working collective?"
(in percentage)

Answer	
People began to look for another job without waiting for dismissal.	31
Alienation has increased among people; people think only of themselves.	30
Conflicts have arisen because of increased competition for one's job.	22
Many people started to get closer to bosses and sought their aid.	20
People became more tolerant to one another.	8
The collective has become more united.	5
Collective actions against firing are being organized.	2
Do not know or question not answered.	30

Source: VCIOM Monitor of working people, Apr. 1993.
Note: Total exceeds 100% because respondents could choose more than one answer.

vide new jobs for the people. It will be some time before the people of Russia become used to the idea that a certain level of unemployment is inevitable, an important trait of a market economy. In the summer of 1993 when the official level of unemployment was 1 percent of employable population, the public attitudes toward the permissibility of unemployment was as follows: 29 percent believed that "unemployment in our country is inadmissible;" 22 percent considered unemployment in the country quite permissible; another 19 percent felt that "limited unemployment is useful;" and 10 percent thought that "unemployment is necessary for effective management of the economy." Twenty percent did not have an opinion.[29]

Even though many theoretically are ready to accept unemployment as an inevitable aspect of life, its menace, along with other economic hardships, is intensifying the discontent with reforms and deepening the criticism and mistrust of government.

Back to Capitalism?

Is Russia moving back to capitalism? It is a question often asked in public debates, in the press, and by political opponents of the reformers. And some people, especially the older generations, are saying bitterly but firmly, "yes—we are ignoring our historical development, forgetting socialist gains, and embracing a faulty sociopolitical system that we rejected and criticized for so many years."

Others, primarily the young people, are answering "yes" with the same firmness: the socialist system is dying, and we are returning to the capitalist path, from which Russia was pushed off by political adventurers seven decades ago.

And some are saying, "we are not moving backward but forward because we are building an enlightened capitalism at the end of the twentieth century, not the capitalism of the century's beginning." In Russia, a regulated market economy is being created, also a welfare state of laws, a state void of ideological labels, and a state that has become part of the civilized world community.

But for the majority of the population it is not clear what is going on. The unfolding events look chaotic. The typical citizen observes the destruction of a familiar world not very affluent but whose existence seemed sound and stable. People do not know what the final result of all this will be, but they realize that for five, ten, or more years an improvement in the economy and their life will not take place.

The people are weighing the results of perestroika and other radical changes, which have taken place since 1985 when Mikhail Gorbachev came to power. In the public's view, it appears that all the problems, which the reforms were supposed to cure, have reached the dimension of crises.

What is happening is called by some people a transition to the market economy, others term it capitalism, but for the majority what is going on is a growing disorder and chaos—and it is ugly and disgusting. Thirty to 38 percent are stating in the polls that they prefer an economy based on the state planning and distribution of the earlier years, as compared to an equal number who chose market economy and private property, while one-quarter to one-third have not thought in those terms but simply dislike what they experience every day.

Regardless of how they rate the pros and cons of the market economy, people don't like the capitalism or the kind of market economy being built in Russia. Besides the fact that most people became poorer and can hardly make ends meet, most citizens feel indignant about the rapidly growing material inequality. The standard of living for the majority of citizens has dropped substantially, compared to what it was before the radical reforms, and one-fifth of the population lives below the poverty line.

According to official statistics, combined income of the upper 10 percent of the population in 1993 was eleven times higher than the income of the lowest 10 percent, as compared to a 4.5 times difference in 1991.[30]

This inequality is constantly monitored in public opinion surveys. Seventy-five percent feel the income distribution is unjust throughout society, and only 9 percent consider it just.[31] More than 70 percent believe that there are more rich people now, and 80 percent think that there are more poor people than a few years ago.

It is hard not to notice this condition. One of the features of early capitalism in Russia is a defiant luxury and self-indulgence among the nouveau riche. People feel enmity and hatred toward the 20-year-old tradesmen driving Mercedeses and BMWs. The new entrepreneurs seem to set about irritating the plain folk with their clothing, their behavior, and even their manner of speech.

Generally, the kind of capitalism observed by most people is the small retail street trade, the kiosks and stalls selling expensive foreign soft drinks and liqueurs, sweets, cigarettes, and appliances and out of reach for ordinary people. Or they resold goods, which they buy at regular stores, at much higher prices.

The controversial and unstable laws that regulate the economy and the exorbitant taxes on private business have led first to the development of trade and shadow businesses, using a minimum investment that exports profits abroad. There was a point in 1992–93 when there were more commodity exchanges in Russia than in any other country in the world.

Those few business people who build brickyards, or produce farming equipment, or manufacture children clothing are not visible to the ordinary person, and they become invisible within a new class of mainly trade businessmen.

For most of the population the advance of capitalism is associated with extensive spread of the rackets, which in reality is controlling most of the businesses and in turn is supervised by major organized criminal groups. And in the minds of a public horrified by the growth of crime, it is the result of the Union's breakup, the collapse of the socialist state, and the development of market economy. The statistics show that public fear of crime is well-founded: the number of murders in 1993 grew 27 percent from the previous year and reached twenty-nine thousand.

In the opinion of most people, it is impossible to get rich by honest means. Speaking about qualities most distinctive of Russian entrepreneurs, 58 percent mentioned the "quest of easy profit," 40 percent the "inclination to cheating and machinations," and 31 percent the "unwillingness to work honestly." Only 23 percent mentioned "business skills."[32]

To a differently worded question, "what leads to wealth most often?" 79 percent picked "good connections," 75 percent "an economic system, which allows rich people to get richer at the expense of the poor," and 72 percent mentioned "dishonesty." Only 46 percent cited a good education, 42 percent gifts and talents, 33 percent luck, and 30 percent hard work.[33] (Respondents could give more than one answer.)

In the opinion of the majority of people, a swindling or Wild West capitalism is being built in Russia with entrepreneurs more resembling outlaws than the honest, noble merchants of prerevolutionary Russia.

Most people think that, as a result of reform, the bulk of property will wind up in the hands of a small group of dishonest people. For instance in a 1993 summer poll, 74 percent believed that most of the state property will fall into the hands of a small group of people because of the privatization program, and only 11 percent thought that it would come into the possession of broad masses of people, as promised by the government.[34]

Various groups of people are united by the idea that something is irreparably broken in the system and that there is no turning back. But at the same time, half of the public feels nostalgic for the past and believes, "it would have been better if everything stayed the way it was before 1985." Possibly it is similar to a nostalgia for one's youth—if only we could stay young. But neither is possible.

The population was entering the reforms of the late 1980s with promises from perestroika leaders that freeing prices during a transition to self-regulating market laws would be quite painless for people; some prices would go up slightly, others down slightly. Of course, all prices jumped substantially and the standard of living fell.

And in general, economic reforms were developing by the worst possible scenario: without a plan or clear understanding of the stages of transformation and without explaining to the people what they should expect. Instead of "shock therapy," the public received the shock without therapy. Therefore, attitudes of the public to economic reform can be compared to attitudes about a painful surgical operation: it hurts horribly, but since you have started, please don't stop!

The majority of the people disapprove of governmental action and Yeltsin's performance as the President. But at the same time, at the April 1993 referendum, the same majority gave Yeltsin a vote of confidence, and, contrary to most predictions, they even supported the so-unloved economic policy of Yeltsin's government.

The majority regrets that the radical changes affecting their daily lives were ever started, but in a ratio of 4 to 3 they support continuation of reforms and generally urge faster, more resolute changes. All this can hardly be called a deeply felt support of economic reforms along a capitalist path; nor can it be called a rejection of socialism. Rather it is a desire of a people, who have lost an ideology, to break away from the deepest crisis by the shortest possible way, under any slogans, hoping that the slogans will work.

6

Moral Standards at a Time of Change

The moral standards with which the population of Russia (and other parts of the old Union) enter the realm of liberal democracy and free enterprise present a strange and generally depressive picture. Foreigners coming to Russia these days are appalled by the increasing amounts of stealing, swindling, and open and disguised racketeering by private individuals and government bureaucrats. And this matter affects not just the growth of crime, typical for many developing countries but something that the Soviet Union did not have to face in the last decades. The nature and character of so many types of crime lead one to believe that a grave illness has afflicted society.

Three examples of these offences against the law have symbolic significance for our discussion.

As reported by the weekly *Moscow News* in May 1993, an emergency situation was created at the Moscow-Volga Canal system, the largest system in the world, because the people of the nearby towns and villages were regularly stealing navigation lights from embankments and waterways. This condition made navigation extremely dangerous and often impossible. People were stealing miniature bulbs and batteries from the signs for home use.[1] Reflection signs and other forms of lighting along the highways often met with a similar fate, and this behavior is indicative of the people's relationship to public property and to the ex-socialist state in general.

Another example is from St. Petersburg, reported in the daily newspaper *Izvestiya,* where the retail trade in all twenty-two boroughs of the city is controlled by the mafia, a condition that likely affects most of the major population centers in Russia.[2]

A third example concerns a rather common situation in the countryside. Members of a collective farm, still the predominant socialist form of agricultural organization, had blinded the cow of a private farmer who settled nearby because the yield of milk that the farmer received from his cow was much higher than what the other farmers received from their cows in the kolkhoz dairy. And the farmer had demonstrated the wonders of enterprise and effectiveness.[3] This act stands out for its outrageous cruelty toward an innocent animal. But also quite common are situations where kolkozniks burn down the private farmers' houses or harm them some other way, and in the process they demonstrate their lack of moral standards and their disgust with the idea of private property.

The rapid growth of criminal activity, vandalism, and violence is a reflection of a deep moral crisis within the Russian society, and it presents a greater danger to the future of the country—as well as to its neighbors—than economic chaos and political instability.

The sudden and unusual nature of the country's moral decay, which coincided with the period of perestroika, suggests that the causes of this decay are connected to radical political and economic reform, and to the rapid transition to a market economy and to the capitalist economic system. It is true that the shock of change, which has torn apart the Union, knocked the communist party from its pedestal, and brought the economy to crisis, has also shaken the moral foundations of the society. But the roots of the moral crisis lay deeper and are connected to the very nature of the departing system.

For seven decades the moral principles evolving from the communist doctrine were intertwined with juridical principles or a special system of laws called the socialist law. Both were based on the power of the state and its punitive organs and were enhanced by repression and fear. Some of these laws penetrated deeply into mass consciousness; others were followed only formally in public, while one's own morality was used around immediate family or in the presence of other families. Moreover, some official standards of morality and of law, which were executed by force, had adverse effects; they boomeranged by creating a subculture of inner opposition to official beliefs—a second stratum of moral behavior. The participants were often hybrids, no longer socialist but not yet fully humanitarian or Christian. This split in the mass consciousness has especially intensified in the last decade, with the hypocrisy and double standards of the ruling elite becoming more and more conspicuous.

A more important result of these "official" moral standards and their reflection in juridical principles was the perpetuation of anomie for seven decades, an alienation and cruelty that became an integral part of society and whose character will be examined next.

Birthmarks of the System

Probably the most important principle in Soviet morality and law was the supremacy of the interests of state and society over the interests of the individual. This fundamental principle had many facets. During the revolution class struggle was proclaimed the motor of history, and the interests of the proletariat were placed above all others, including group or personal concerns. The world was divided into proletarians and the enemies of the proletariat, and the latter group was most vulnerable to extermination. In more peaceful times the fervor of this rhetoric would cool down but the fundamental belief always remained: "all efforts for the good of society;" "self-denying labor for the Motherland—a duty of each citizen." Any person or group ignoring this principle was severely stigmatized or punished. In the 1930s tardiness at work three times would result in trial; nonfulfillment of a work quota could lead to the loss of personal rights for food rationing cards; in the 1960s and the 1970s, "parasitism," the evasion of work "for the good of society," was punishable as a criminal offense.

The system had a certain consistency: whole-hearted obedience of its citizens to society and to the state was supposed to be rewarded with the state's care of the plain folks. A relevant maxim declared that the chief goal of the socialist state was to "fully satisfy the growing material and cultural needs of the Soviet people."

Self-denial, i.e., voluntarily self-limiting interests in the name of society, was reinforced with patriotic motives: serving the state and society also meant devotion to the Socialist Motherland. This two-fold propagandistic strategy allowed the morality of self-denial to spread far and wide in the name of a collective or larger group. The very concept of "serving" was deeply rooted in mass psychology and is still evident in the behavior of elder generations. Often the object of serving lost its clear shape and embodied a voluntary reluctance or fear to present personal demands, interests, or points of view. Fortified with a Russian peasant commune psychology, these ideas have become an integral part of the personality of the "homo sovieticus."

At the same time, after the war and especially in the 1960s and the 1970s, a protest began to grow among part of the population against the personality's continued suppression by the state, and the thaw of the 1960s offered prospect for a broader discussion, in the press, in literature, and in the arts, of individual rights and the importance and integrity of private lives. Probably the severest blow to the psychology of state paternalism, self-denying service, and the "caring" state headed by the "sage" leader was dealt by the exposure of Stalinist repressions, mass executions, and the deaths of millions in the gulag camps. After these disclosures at the Twentieth Party Congress, any harmony between the personality and the state was doomed and would never be recovered even by the true adherents of socialism.

Even more devastating was the effect of the false propaganda about the caring state. The ideals of a simple life could no longer conceal the obvious hypocrisy and open hedonism of the ruling elite, especially among youth. In contrast to the official dogma of self-denial, its antipode was spreading—limitless egoism and contempt not only for the interests of abstract society but also for individual persons or types, i.e., social Darwinism in its cruelest form—contempt for the weak and less fortunate. This attitude became quite obvious in the 1960s and the 1970s, when a condescending cynicism, if not a mass contempt, began to spread to the official ideology and morals. It was treated with all the regard one has for an inevitable evil, as with a uniform, uncomfortable but accepted by society.

This other "real" morality—in contrast to the official one—presupposed the perennial truths: "the stronger one survives," "one should take care of oneself." Consequently, a related double work ethic was growing: working just to mark time or to do things by halves for the state offset by a much more intense and effective work for oneself, on an unofficial contract for cash without paying taxes. Alongside the official morality of self-denial, this other morality was growing stronger: it included theft from the state and a contempt for everything emanating from the state and its institutions.

Another belief propagated within the Soviet nation since the revolution was the supremacy of the sacred socialist property, i.e., the promotion of state or government property and the negation of private property. The revolution had taken the means of production from the private owners, and then for seven decades the government had perpetuated a belief in the inviolability of state property using propaganda, the law, and the force of repression. Of the three tools, repression was the most effective; for example, in the 1930s, people were sent to slave labor camps for picking up stalks of wheat left in the fields after harvesting. After the war, when fear of repression had gradually subsided, the theft of state property began to grow quickly.

In spite of the propaganda (and contrary to it), a belief was entrenched in the mass consciousness that state-owned and, in general, publicly owned property actually meant nobody's property and, therefore, you could take whatever you wanted. A post-war socialism had introduced into the Soviet reality and the Russian language the concept of *nesun*. This practice was and still is a mass "carrying out"—theft by the employees from their respective enterprises of everything that was produced there: candies from the sweets factory, meat from the meat plant, instruments and spare parts from the machine-building plants. The stolen goods carried out were hidden under garments, thrown over the fences, or taken out on trucks. There were cases where inventive workers pumped alcohol into truck tires and drove it out of the factories. No inspection would find it. Frequently, the guards, who had been bribed, cooperated by looking the other way.

What is especially important here for the present mass psychology is the fact that communist propaganda has failed to create an idol of the state property. Indeed, throughout decades of oppression, the activity of the communist press, along with literature and the arts, has created in the population a lack of respect for private property. You can take something owned by the state because it actually belongs to nobody. And to steal from a private person is also not so bad because the goods were probably acquired by dishonest means anyway. Obviously, the poor are being robbed too, but in a mass culture the contempt for all things "private"—for "petty bourgeoisie proprietary instinct" and for "bourgeoisie consumerism"—was widely spread. The Leninist slogan from revolutionary times, "rob the robbers," has remained in the mass consciousness until now. The double standard about property in the penal code helps support this belief: much more severe punishment was envisaged for stealing socialist property than for looting individuals.

The consequences of this phenomenon are being strongly felt now during the period of radical economic reform. More and more people are developing a taste for acquiring property and for owning land or businesses but the majority still do not have enough respect for the property belonging to someone else. Consequently, there has been an unprecedented increase in the theft of both public and private property by ex-socialists, and by the new "bourgeoisie." The slogan, "rob the robbers," has achieved a second life.

An important role in molding the Soviet system of moral principles and mass morality was played by the principle of law subordination, legal standards, and juridical education to the political ideology. The totalitarian system declared that the law should serve class and proletarian interests and made it an inviolate rule. Anything that strengthened the dictatorship of the proletariat was just. This theory was used as a justification for repression. Consequently, over the years this practice has subordinated the role of the courts to the political institutions, the commissars, and the party chiefs at all levels. A postwar version of it was the so-called "telephone law," when a party or a Soviet chieftain would call a judge, an investigator, or a prosecutor and advise him about what decision to make.

Despite all the speculation in propagandistic literature (meant for Western consumption) that the Soviet law was based on the Roman law or on international legal principles, domestically the people were told that the foundation of Russian law was the proletarian, class, and socialist law consciousness.

The result of this indoctrination was two-fold. On the one hand, three generations of people have grown up believing that the legal principles and laws should be different—one set for the proletarians and "the working people," and one for the "representatives of the exploiter classes." These people accepted quite naturally the deprivation of these "representatives" of electoral rights in the 1920s. On the other hand, because the laws are being interpreted by the bosses on the basis of their proletarian consciousness, abiding by the laws is not absolute or inviolable. It is more important to understand whether certain laws are useful to the society, the revolution, or the authorities.

Again, because the laws depend so much on the ruling elite, when the respect for this elite drops so does the fear of, and obedience to, the laws emanating from these agencies of power. This trend blossomed after Stalin's death, existed during Khruschev's tenure, and has persisted until 1993. Thus the impudent behavior of the Bolsheviks, who used these laws, boomeranged and became a kind of legal nihilism for the population.

This nihilism created by the Soviet system has fallen onto the fertile soil of traditional Russian belief which treats law as secondary in importance to the principle of justice. The Russian mentality has traditionally divided the laws into just, good, and right (those which should be obeyed) and incorrect and unjust (those which may not be so strictly observed). Observance of the laws in Russia has never been automatic.

This hybrid behavior creating a Russian-Soviet legal nihilism will continue for a long time to foster crime in the country and obstruct the transition to the rule of law as promised by the democratic reformers.

One more joint product developed over the seven Soviet decades is the Russian-Soviet authoritarianism of personality, and this too will have an adverse effect on establishing civilized moral principles and the democratization of social institutions and of the mass consciousness.

The molding of an authoritarian personality in Russia was furthered by the monarchy, by serfdom, and by the Russian Orthodox traditions. In turn, the continuation of these institutions was based to a great degree on the widely spread authoritarianism of the people.

The Bolshevik revolution had substituted Leninist-Stalinist despotism for the monarchy, and the Soviet totalitarian system created an ideal environment for the development of authoritarian qualities found in the public. This combined traditional and Soviet authoritarianism was characterized by ideological and political intolerance, conformity, devotion to the idea of a strong leader (in the family, in a small group or organization, or in the entire state), the spread of anti-semitism, and the lack of appreciation for equality and women's rights. Authoritarian thinking for a considerable part of the population is the reserve of conservatism and resides with the proponents of totalitarian restoration.

Another important quality found in the departing system continues to live in the mass consciousness. Whatever Soviet propaganda said about the humanitarian nature of the socialist system (its orientation toward the interests of all people and not to the wishes of a financial oligarchy, as in the West), much of it was superficial and the system regularly demonstrated to its subjects its cruel and repressive disposition. Although diminished in the 1960s, the killing of millions of people and the continuation of mass repressions were still present in the public's mind as a draconian educational tool of the system. The criminal penitentiary system was arranged in such a way to cripple the people morally and turn out recidivists, which still continues to this day.

Another institution well known as a breeding ground of cruelty was the army where, especially since the 1970s, the beating and humiliation of soldiers in the first year of service by their elder peers have become customary, the so-called *dedovschina*—from the word for "grandfather."

Most institutions of the Soviet era were created in such a way to disparage the personality and suppress a person's independence and personal dissent. This condition alienated the people from the state and from one another; it also promoted an intolerance and cruelty directed at members of other social and ethnic groups and at animals—it represented a general brutality, caddishness, and disdain toward others.

The endless and hypocritical declarations by officials on the humaneness and brotherhood of the Soviet people also had an adverse effect on public morality. These slogans and declarations about the friendships among the indigenous peoples of the Soviet Union, however beautiful and noble they seemed, came to be rejected more and more by the public in the last two decades as hypocritical. The public perceived these statements as springing from a system that was being increasingly criticized for its official mendacity about morals and ideology.

The breakdown of the Soviet totalitarian system and the withdrawal of the communist party as a ruling power have also, to a great extent, led to the destruction of a set of moral values associated with this political and ideological system. Whatever merits this system of moral values had, it collapsed with the collapse of socialism. And no system of values was offered in its place. The religious value system was destroyed by the Communist regime even earlier—directly after the Revolution. This too has contributed to the current conditions. As the result of all this, a moral vacuum has been formed in a country transitioning to a market economy and a democracy.

The moral climate in Russia during this transitional period is filled with mass anomie, moral decay, and legal nihilism. It is a period represented by permissiveness approaching anarchy, public alienation from society and from each other, and authoritarian traits of cruelty and violence. And these conditions in turn breed all types of crime. Certainly, crime also has developed in other countries during periods of economic crisis. But the breeding ground for crime in Russia at this time of radical change can be found in the moral degradation of society, the result of seven decades of communist dictatorship.

Human Nature and Alienation

Different aspects of this moral crisis are reflected in the mass public polling of recent years, specifically, the VCIOM polls and the surveys of the present author on morality and crime. In the major study of summer 1990, details about the psychological climate during the period of radical reforms were studied, including mass views on right and wrong and moral and amoral behavior. One topic was thoroughly investigated: to what extent are altruistic and egoistic inclinations common in the mass public? What is the level of alienation among people? A question of the survey was: "in your opinion, do most people think about others? Are they ready to help or do they care mostly about

Table 6.1

"Do most people think about others and are they willing to help them, or do they care mostly about themselves and are not concerned about others?"

(in percentage)

Answer	Russia	Ukraine	Baltic	Caucasus	Middle Asia
Think about others	13	11	11	22	12
Care only about themselves	69	73	68	61	67
Difficult to answer	18	16	21	17	21

Source: N. Popov, "Morality, Crime, and Law Enforcement," VCIOM report, June 1990.

themselves and are not concerned about others?" The great majority, 70 percent, thought that people were concerned only about themselves, and only 13 percent believed that people cared about others and were ready to help. Eighteen percent had no definite opinion on this subject.[4]

Because this poll was one of the last surveys on the subject conducted in the USSR, comparison of the Russian results with responses from the other republics is useful at this point (see table 6.1).

Thus with all the cultural and religious differences throughout the various geographic and ethnic regions of the Soviet Union, the common political and socioeconomic processes within the communist empire have created and shaped a similar moral climate of prevailing relationships among people. Unfortunately, there were no public opinion polls conducted in previous decades, and we can not trace the dynamics of this relationship. The only similar poll, with questions worded somewhat differently, demonstrated in 1989 that 56 percent nationwide believed that "people only care about their own advantages; they are indifferent to the fate of others," while 35 percent were of the opinion that "people care not only about themselves but try to help others too."[5]

A more general approach to human nature was used in another question and examined whether conflicts and wars were an integral part of human nature (see table 6.2).

People in the Caucasus obviously have numerous reasons to believe in the ineradicability of conflicts and wars. But throughout the rest of the nation, 40 percent thought that aggressiveness is an integral part of

Table 6.2
"Do you agree with the statement that human nature is such that there will always be conflicts and wars?"
(in percentage)

Answer	Average (for USSR)	Russia	Ukraine	Baltic	Caucasus	Middle Asia
Agree	40	38	38	47	60	45
Disagree	40	42	42	31	27	35
Difficult to answer	20	20	20	22	13	20

Source: N. Popov, "Morality, Crime, and Law Enforcement," VCIOM report, June 1990.

human nature. Therefore, "one should always be ready to counter aggression, care about oneself, and not trust people too much." The matter of trust was specifically addressed in a number of polls. In the survey mentioned above, 54 percent said that "most people can be trusted," and 37 percent believed to the contrary that you cannot be too careful dealing with people.[6] Comparing these results with similar American polling data of the same period gave the following results:

(in percentage)	USSR	USA
People care only about themselves	70	45
Most people cannot be trusted	37	34

A number of questions have been used in different countries to gauge an individual's level of alienation in society, whether they be feelings of helplessness or conditions where civil rights or a moral value system may be lacking. In the survey mentioned above one such scale was used, that of H. McClosky and J. H. Schaar. Results of the responses are given in table 6.3, along with results from the American polls (the U.S. study was done in the mid-1960s).[7]

As the table shows, some results are very similar, especially those results dealing with emotional attitudes. Other values relating to societal changes are substantially higher in the USSR, and generally the mean level of alienation is higher there as well—62 percent, while in the U.S. it was 48 percent. These results suggest a breakdown within

Table 6.3

Statements on Alienation

(percentage in agreement)

Statements	USSR	USA
Many things which our fathers believed in are being destroyed right before our eyes.	82	48
Everything is so unstable now it seems anything might happen.	81	82
The problem now is that most people do not believe in anything at all.	74	44
In the present state of confusion and disorder, it is hard to understand in what to believe.	70	50
Everything is changing so quickly now that it is hard to understand which laws to follow.	65	49
What we lack now is a true friendship for life (as it used to be).	64	69
In the past people used to feel better because everyone knew what was the right thing to do.	51	27
Often I feel at a loss and out of place.	41	37
It seems to me that others know better than I what is right and what is wrong.	33	27

Source: N. Popov, "Morality, Crime, and Law Enforcement," VCIOM report, June 1990; H. McClosky and J. H. Schaar, "Psychological Dimensions of Anomie," *American Sociological Review* 30 (1965): 14–40.

the established institutions of an entire way of life during a period of fundamental societal restructuring.

The survey results reveal noticeable differences in attitudes throughout the different regions of the Soviet Union. With a mean level of 62 percent, the results are somewhat higher in Russia and the Ukraine, somewhat lower in Byelorussia and Middle Asia (56 and 57 percents), and much lower in the Baltic republics (48 percent, and similar to the U.S. level). (See table 6.4.)

No one social group appears to be significantly more alienated than any other. The level of alienation is slightly lower among the better educated and those older persons having a higher job status or qualification. Women are more alienated than men. Alienation is highest in the age group of 30 to 55.

Table 6.4
Statements on Alienation in Regions of the USSR
(percentage in agreement)

	Average (for USSR)	Russia	Ukraine	Baltic	Caucuses	Middle Asia
Many things which our fathers believed in are being destroyed right before our eyes.	82	87	84	62	79	68
Everything is so unstable now it seems anything might happen.	81	84	77	80	83	76
In the present state of confusion and disorder, it is hard to understand in what to believe.	70	73	70	58	74	57
What we lack now is a true friendship for life (as it used to be).	64	68	67	55	48	63

Source: N. Popov, "Morality, Crime, and Law Enforcement," VCIOM report, June 1990.

Personal attitudes toward different moral beliefs were also addressed. In particular, respondents were asked to express their attitude to the well-known Christian maxim "do unto others what you want others to do unto you." The answers were as follows: "this is the only way one should live," 49 percent; "this is unrealistic," 17 percent; "in today's world it is impossible to live like that," 17 percent; "too difficult to answer," 16 percent.[8]

This principle, therefore, was rejected as useless or unrealistic by a third of the population. The attitudes of those believing in God were practically the same as those of the atheists: the principle was rejected by 39 percent of the Muslims and 32 percent of the Christians. There was a marked difference in the answers coming from various geographical regions; the maxim was rejected by only 24 percent of the respondents from the Baltic republics and by 46 percent from Middle Asia. Even more important, among all age groups rejection was the highest among the youth: 46 percent of the 20–24 age group rejected the principle, and only 37 percent accepted it.

The prevalence of anomie in society was assessed through answers to a common question raised in public discussions about personal morality (see table 6.5): "some people say, especially the young ones, that all talks about morality, decency, and generosity are deceit and hypocrisy, and in reality everyone is concerned only with oneself, and if you trip, you get trodden on." In Russia, 25 percent shared this view, 40 percent believed that some people are really following this rule, and only 25 percent had the opinion that "most people are kind and decent, and it is wrong to think that way about them."

These views reveal a realistic but regrettable perception of the actual moral conditions in society. In general, public opinion results and other observations show that for the substantial part of the population in Russia and in other areas of the former Soviet Union (close to one-half) an erosion or deterioration of these moral values is a typical belief, and these same people doubt that such a system is still working in the society. Moreover, one-quarter of the population simply rejects any system of universal humanitarian, socialist, or religious moral belief. And this moral deterioration has not been slowed by the restoration of religion as a legitimate institution or by the growth in the number of believers—45 percent of the people are still atheists.

More than any other group, the youth have quite readily rejected the old socialist ideology, morality, and institutions, and they are professing some kind of homemade set of market or capitalist values acquired mostly from Western movies. These new values serve as a background or as a moral foundation for the peculiar kind of "wild West capitalism" that is developing in Russia today.

These values presuppose harsh competition: all methods are valid; disrespect and hostility are viewed as signs of strength; and threats and violence are common arguments for achieving personal ends.

The Morality of Inequality

The spread of this moral vacuum and anomie is promoted by the growth of social tension produced by a transition from the socialist to market economic structure. Economic and social expectations are set up among the people, never to be realized, and frustration sets in instead. The rise of private businesses with high salaries on the one hand and the decline of most state-owned enterprises with much lower wages on the other (with a general impoverishment affecting most people) has led to a general perception of economic and social inequality and

Table 6.5

"Some people, especially the young, say that all discussions about morality, decency, and generosity are deceit and hypocrisy, and in reality everyone is concerned only with oneself, and if you trip, you get trodden on. What is your opinion on that?"

(in percentage)

Answer	Average (for USSR)	Age 18–29	Age 30–49	Age Over 50	Status Professionals	Status Workers	Regions Russia	Regions Baltic	Regions Middle Asia
This is really so.	24	25	23	22	21	25	25	13	34
Some people really think that way.	39	44	39	37	45	38	40	60	27
It is wrong to think this; what about people?—most of them are kind and decent.	25	19	28	29	26	23	25	23	24
Difficult to answer.	11	12	10	12	8	14	10	5	16

Source: N. Popov, "Morality, Crime, and Law Enforcement," VCIOM report, June 1990.

injustice. Many people still view guaranteed employment, equal pay, and a decent standard of living as their inalienable rights and feel cheated and betrayed by the market conditions. Unable to fulfill their aspirations or to change anything in their lives, they nurture a persistent irritation, indignation, or bitterness, which often turns into acts of social protest or, under other conditions, leads to violence, criminal acts, or vandalism.

This bitterness and rage is often directed against the state and the new government or against any top authority. In other cases it is aimed at different ethnic or religious groups. For many persons, the objects of indignation and hatred are the new businessmen, the speculators or traders—but just as often it can be a hatred aimlessly directed. In any case material inequality is constantly on people's minds, along with the day-by-day financial problems.

Most people feel—and it irritates them—that the income and material goods in society are unequitably and unjustly distributed; this is the opinion of more than 75 to 80 percent.[9]

When asked where they see the main injustice of income distribution, one-third to one-half of the respondents singled out unlawful profiteering, speculation, and corruption. Another third mentioned that some groups get too little, specifically pensioners, disabled people, and single mothers. A sizable portion of the public, therefore, directed their dissatisfaction with uneven income distribution at the new rich, who get their profit unlawfully and unjustly, and at the corrupted bureaucrats.

These feelings of frustration and injustice are fortified by the ideas, spread for decades by the official propaganda, that even though socialism is against leveling, differences in income within the country are minimal. And the ethics of a simple life was cultivated for everyone; it combined voluntary simplicity with asceticism, and it accentuated spiritual, and eschewed material, values. A constant propagandistic and educational struggle was waged against the bourgeois and against their consumerism and materialism.

When this system of socialist-forced equality fell apart, it was a signal for many people that there were no official bans on acquiring those goods, which they secretly desired for so long; they no longer had to hide what they acquired. And so the voluntary simplicity turned into conspicuous consumption and a demonstration to the rest of the world of what they owned.

In the suburbs of large cities, the new villas compete for one's attention with their size and extravagance. Traders in the markets and at the street kiosks are proudly displaying their Toyotas and Mercedeses. This opulence applies to a limited, though quite visible, part of the population, and the rest have to be content with the goods obtained during socialism.

This conspicuous material inequality is now a powerful psychological irritant, pushing some toward constantly striving to achieve the standard of living and material well-being of the newly rich, while driving others to envy, frustration, and hatred of this new class of owners.

The economic policy of the government to promote market reforms is also contributing to the growth of these feelings of frustration. Part of the transition process consists of encouraging independence and initiative in individuals and in collectives for the new market conditions. Many people understand this logic and support it in principle. But at the same time traditional reliance on the state is still strong in the mass consciousness. These conflicting orientations increase confusion and frustration. On the one hand, about 50 percent of the public are of the opinion that "people should take care of themselves and decide what to do to achieve success in life." On the other hand, about 40 percent, by VCIOM's polls, still believe that "the state and the government should be primarily responsible for the success and well-being of people." Often these groups are not two halves of the same public but are comprised of the same people simply taking conflicting or contradictory positions.

Quite possibly, the Russian market economy in the future will develop along the lines of Western liberalism and the welfare state, with a strong social safety net. But what people are seeing now is mainly drastic reduction of social benefits and a free-for-all in economic life. The general tone of any discussion in the media suggests competition, self-reliance, efficiency, and unemployment benefits for industry. On top of the current economic hardships, this is adding insult to injury. People feel betrayed, and this feeling combines with a sense of inequality and frustration and increases alienation.

Authoritarian Personality

Authoritarian traits in the Russian national character were coalescing for ages under the influence of three centuries of Tartar-Mongol occupation and control, followed by monarchy and serfdom, and then by Soviet totalitarianism. Some features of the Russian authoritarian mentality at the turn of the century were described in terms of patriarchal values in the literature of the day, where a grandfather or a father would enjoy implicit authority and obedience. Strict discipline was important in a child's upbringing. Also characteristic were the subordinate and humiliating positions women assumed within the family and society. Also quite typical was the personal respect and esteem directed at all chiefs, senior authorities, or persons in high-ranking positions.

This perception seems to contradict the well-known wild Russian nature—full of carelessness, recklessness, and emotionality—with its disdain for discipline and all the rules. These qualities, nevertheless, coexisted quite easily with a respect for authority directed at a formal or informal group leader—of a workers' artel or a peasants' commune, where relations were based on one-man management. Frequent peasant rebellions were directed not against the authority of the leader per se but against the "bad" tsar and were led by their own tough authoritarian leader, who would often proclaim himself the tsar.

These qualities of traditional Russian authoritarianism were then influenced by the Soviet totalitarian system, with its constant intimidation and terror through the agencies of power. These practices have enforced the old authoritarian stereotypes and developed a reverence to any official, especially to the state and the party chiefs.

The impact of the Soviet system on moral views and values was quite uneven and contradictory, and just as contradictory were the conditions of mass psychology created by it. For instance, the Soviet power structure gave equal rights to women and in different ways was stimulating women's participation in economic and social life. Women received voting privileges and have entered the traditionally male occupations of engineering and medicine. But in politics they numbered only in the dozens, and the Soviet and now Russian post-totalitarian political culture is still dominated by males. In everyday life age-old stereotypes of male supremacy are still widely in effect. People of both sexes would rather speak about "helping" the "fair sex" than of true equality.

In the study of morality and crime mentioned above, the authoritarian inclinations were measured using some of the well-known works by T. W. Adorno, specifically, the modified F Scale.[10] Some of these attitudes are recorded in table 6.6.

As these figures show, authoritarian attitudes prevail, with the exception of the woman's role in politics. Here it should be mentioned that the prowomen trend is probably not a sincere response but represents a desire to follow the formal social principle of equality. Many

Table 6.6
Attitudes about Authoritarianism
(in percentage)

Attitude	Agree	Disagree	Difficult to Answer
The main problem today is that people talk too much and work too little.	80	13	7
What is needed most today for a child's upbringing is strictness and discipline by parents.	66	22	11
A few strong leaders can do more for our country than all the laws and rhetoric.	51	28	21
Most people who fare badly in life simply lack persistence and willpower.	45	32	23
In politics it is better to do without women.	28	56	16

Source: N. Popov, "Morality, Crime, and Law Enforcement," VCIOM report, June 1990.

people in their private attitudes about women follow traditional conservative stereotypes, but in public or when answering general questions, they follow a social cliché. In any case, the number of people with authoritarian attitudes is twice those with the nonauthoritarian mentality.

In authoritarian types among its people, Russia occupies a middle position compared to other parts of the USSR. Ukraine and Byelorus are similar to Russia. As can be construed from earlier chapters, a higher level of authoritarianism exists in the Caucasus and Middle Asia, a lower level in the Baltic states.

Authoritarian traits can be used to measure or examine beliefs or attitudes, including religious intolerance. Not infrequently the consequences of this intolerance are ethnocentricity and racial or ethnic prejudices, including antisemitism, which breaks out periodically in Russia. People with an authoritarian type of personality are more prone to support fascism and communism and not a democratic value system in society.

During the period of reforms in Russia, the presence of authoritarian traits blocked the development of a democratic culture and the creation of democratic institutions. As mentioned in chapter 4, many people were ready to support democracy in principle or as a form of public participation in decision making, free elections, and a parliamentary system. But at the same time they felt nostalgia for the clarity and order of the totalitarian past and were ready to support a "strong leader," even at the expense of curtailing for some time freedom and democracy.

Authoritarian orientations are well pronounced in public attitudes about people with deviant behavior, people violating the law, or people who are social outcasts for some reason. In a number of VCIOM surveys, attitudes about such people were probed, particularly those opinions about what society's role should be in dealing with these people. The choices included to "isolate [them] from society," to "leave [them] alone," and to "provide [them] help." Table 6.7 shows the attitudes toward some of these categories of people.

The data demonstrates how widespread the "rejection reaction" is. It reflects a severe and even repressive intolerance toward people with deviant behavior, excluding murderers. The majority proposed to "isolate from society" the prostitutes and more than 40 percent included drug addicts, homosexuals, and people ill with AIDS. One-third proposed to isolate from society all mentally ill persons and "rockers," young unruly motorcycle riders. One-fifth would isolate tramps and people with birth defects. These results suggest that people are advocating the isolation and imprisonment of all those whose behavior, way of life, or appearance is unacceptable or unpleasant to them, without ever examining whether these people violated the law or whether the proposed measures correspond to perceived deviations from a value system or set of laws.

This intolerance is more prevalent among the older generations and the less educated, but it has also spread among the youth. For example, more than one-third of the young people below 25 (including college students) propose to isolate homosexuals and drug addicts from society—and one-quarter from this group people with birth defects.

In a 1989 VCIOM survey, when a similar set of questions was first asked about the same groups of deviants and the option "to liquidate" was offered, the results revealed that one-third suggested liquidation of homosexuals, about one-quarter the prostitutes and drug addicts, and one-fifth the rockers and people with birth defects.[11] The present author did not use this alternative in the survey question because it was too provocative and too difficult to interpret the responses of those choosing this option. But as an emotional reaction to people "not like us," it is quite indicative.

Table 6.7
"There are people in our society whose appearance and behavior deviate from acceptable standards. In your opinion, how should these people be treated?"
(in percentage)

Group	Isolate from Society	Provide Help	Leave Alone	Difficult to Answer
Murderers	92	3	1	4
Homosexuals	47	10	18	25
Drug Addicts	43	45	3	9
Prostitutes	42	11	22	25
People Ill with AIDS	42	50	2	6
Mentally Ill People	33	59	1	7
Rockers	30	11	28	32
People with Birth Defects	20	60	3	17
Tramps	19	52	10	19
Alcoholics	19	62	7	12
Hippies	13	10	40	37
Members of Religious Sects	8	7	57	28
Beggars	4	82	5	9

Source: N. Popov, "Morality, Crime, and Law Enforcement," VCIOM report, June 1990.

Some of the attitudes toward different minorities are changing as society becomes more democratized and a growing permissiveness becomes more acceptable. Prostitution is widely spread and almost legal. Homosexuality is no longer a criminal offense as it once was during the Soviet era. Drug use and drug trafficking is rapidly increasing. Sexual customs are quite different from those of the early 1980s. But that applies primarily to major cities and the younger age groups. For the majority of the population, traditional intolerance is still very common.

Law Offenders: Pros and Amateurs

The severe economic crisis, the weakening of all organs of power including the judiciary, and the moral degradation of society all have contributed to the uncontrollable growth of crime in Russia. According to the Ministry of Internal Affairs, 533,000 were serving sentences in "corrective labor camps" and prisons in the summer of 1993. Another 239,000 convicted persons were working outside colonies at construction and in industry under police supervision. Under investigation and kept in investigatory confinement were another 210,000 people. The sum of these groups represents about one million criminals and persons charged with crimes.

Of those convicted, 60 percent committed more than one crime; one-quarter were convicted of premeditated murder or inflicting serious bodily injuries; one-fifth each convicted of armed robbery, burglary, and rape. One-half of all convicts committed violent assaults on people.[12] By all assessments most of those serving time are really dangerous criminals.

More important than the sheer size of the prison population is the rapidly growing crime rate and the fact that most crimes go undetected. For the five years from 1989 to 1993, the number of crimes in Russia has doubled. For instance, in 1992 more than 2,761,000 crimes were registered but only 647,000 criminals were convicted. More than two-thirds of all crimes went unpunished.[13]

Of all personal property thefts which comprise about 40 percent of registered crimes, only 20 percent are detected. No more than one-third of most other crimes are detected, by official estimates.[14] Estimates from the public are even more pessimistic.

From the results of public opinion polling, 48 percent of Moscovites became victims of crimes during the five-year period from 1988 to 1992. One-half of the victims did not report the crime to the police because "they would not be able to do anything due to lack of evidence," because "the police would not want to help," or for other reasons.[15] From a 1990 survey, 25 percent have been victims of violent assault at some time in their life during a robbery, rape attempt, hooliganism, etc.[16] A survey from fall 1991 has shown that 30 percent became victims of one or more crimes over the previous two years.[17]

From the survey of the State Statistics Committee in 1991, 70 percent of the people do not feel secure using public transportation in the evenings, and 34 percent do not in the daytime. Seventy-eight percent do not feel safe in the streets at night and 31 percent do not during the daytime. Finally, even at home people do not consider it quite safe—38 percent at night and 18 percent during the day.[18]

Consequently, 70 percent of the public report that they are concerned about criminal acts against their families or themselves, and 30 percent have "grave concerns." In the lists of problems that "bother people most" (asked in many polls), crime occupies second place after concerns of sky-rocketing prices and impoverishment.

If we combine the official statistics with the public's assessments the result would be several million criminal acts committed annually. By some estimates about 30 million people convicted for crimes have passed through the penitentiary system over the last two to three decades. In some areas there are difficulties in finding people for administrative positions who don't have some criminal record. It turns out that about one-third of the adult population are law offenders or criminals, and one-half of the adult population were victims of criminal acts over the last five years.

However the prevalence of crime is measured, the picture is threatening. The President certainly understood the perilous situation when he said in the summer of 1993 that "criminality is developing into the state problem today; it undermines the process of reform and the economic foundations of our state."[19] Even more alarming is the condition described by B. Yerin, Minister of Internal Affairs: "We are dealing here with not just organized crime but a criminal aggression aimed at the stability of society and at the constitutional structure of our state. . . . In fact, what is going on is the merging of general, economic, and organized crime. And if we do not undertake decisive measures immediately, the state will be subdivided into spheres of influence. The mafia structures will become the real rulers."[20] The Minister believes "it would be wrong to consider this situation the result of the reforms going on for the last two to three years. An unbiased analysis shows that we are reaping the results of the legal nihilism that became more acute as far back as the 80s."[21]

The legal nihilism mentioned by the Minister suggests a widespread anomie, a breakdown of moral values, and a casual if not contemptuous attitude toward the law. In the opinion of a growing number of Russian citizens, the laws are just as unjust as is the rest of society. Moreover, the system or the state creating these laws has collapsed, and the new system is hardly any better; therefore, there is no reason to observe those laws.

The fabric of the mass consciousness is quite complicated: when "others" are in question—criminals, speculators, greedy businessmen, and corrupted bureaucrats—the laws should be made more severe and be strictly enforced. If the people themselves are involved, those suffering at the hands of criminals or the merciless state are not obligated to follow all the laws.

This complicated attitude is demonstrated in the polls too. VCIOM survey in December 1990 posed this question to address the problem: "should all laws be observed without exception, or should one sometimes act according to one's conscience?" Thirty-four percent believed that the laws should be observed without exception, while 53 percent thought that sometimes one should act according to one's conscience. Thirteen percent had no opinion on the issue, which is also significant; apparently two-thirds of the public reserve the right to decide for themselves whether to observe the laws or not.[22]

Quite significant are the answers to another question: "can one live in the Soviet Union without breaking the law?" Only 29 percent think that one can; 50 percent believe that it is impossible, and 19 percent had no answer.[23] It does not necessarily follow from the answers that only 29 percent observe the laws, but these answers are quite characteristic of the moral climate.

One consequence of this general indifference to the law is the growth of widespread economic violations. For decades many people were purchasing illegally—that is, obtaining consumer goods under the counter or at the black market or overpaying for scarce commodities. In a poll 28 percent revealed that they were doing it constantly, 56 percent said that they were involved in this practice occasionally, and only 18 percent claimed that they never had to do it.[24]

Also important in this regard are attitudes toward bribing officials and administrators of all levels. Thirteen percent confessed in the poll that they have to regularly give bribes in the form of money, gifts, and other favors. Twenty-eight percent said they have to do it but rather rarely. Another 22 percent believed that there are situations when this is needed, but they just don't know how to do it. Only 31 percent said they are not doing anything like that out of principle.[25]

With the beginning of the transition to market economy and the emergence of a class of entrepreneurs, the corruption of officials and bureaucrats has reached unprecedented heights. A portion of each day in a new businessman's schedule is spent getting permission from one or another state agency, which must sign some document or paper. And every such act costs and must be paid for. One example shows how this practice spreads. At a conference of entrepreneurs in Bashkiria, a republic within the Russian Federation, a sociological poll of the participants was conducted. Fifty percent of the businessmen reported in the poll that they have to give bribes continuously to local and republican agencies of power.[26]

Often even with bribes, an entrepreneur cannot overcome those barriers to business activity erected by bureaucrats at all levels of state control—barriers that include a hardened, inflexible system of economic laws and regulations. Most businessmen have to bend and violate those laws constantly. In a certain way, the reproaches from the people—that the new money is acquired dishonestly—are justified, even though most businessmen are indignant at the practice.

The belief that it is hardly possible to do anything in the country now without violating certain laws is shown in responses to another poll. Fifty-four percent believe that "in our life today one can hardly solve an important problem without using illegal ways, even though it evokes internal protest." Twenty-six percent did not agree with that position.[27]

One unlawful way to solve one's financial or material problems has already been mentioned: "carry out"—petty theft of one's own production at plants, shops, and farms. In the opinion of 46 percent of the respondents, the majority do not blame those involved in "carry out."[28]

In general, the attitudes of the population toward the theft of state property and toward the constant small bribes and gifts are quite permissive. The majority use these and other justifications during a time of radical reform and economic hardship to explain or rationalize the minor deviations or excusable defects. They seem less significant against the background of serious crimes and decades of injustice at the hands of the state.

The prolonged destruction of Christian or humanitarian morality, followed by the breakdown of a surrogate Soviet morality, has led to a deep moral crisis in the Russian society. This crisis's seriousness is aggravated by the fact that the new political and economic structure of society—the replacement of the party's totalitarianism with the rudiments of democracy in the shape of free elections, parliamentary system, separation of powers, and transition to market economy—could not create by itself and over a short period of time a new ideological or moral system. Any hope for religion to become society's moral educator is in vain because the traditional religions themselves will be restored only over a long period of time.

The disappearance of the Soviet ideological and moral system has led not only to a moral emptiness but also to the destruction of the positive, humanitarian components in the socialist morality because they are associated with the former political system. Many of these principles based on positive qualities of the old system have been turned into their opposite, especially by the youth. Timid attempts of the country's new rulers to introduce democratic values and humanitarian morality have not met with much public support because most people are extremely critical of the government for its practice of economic shock therapy, and they have little trust in any governmental ideas.

Consequently, the territory of the ex-Soviet Union, and especially Russia, has become the breeding ground for criminal activity of all kinds, and this activity will continue to spread to other former Soviet bloc countries as well.

Even if the disorganized economy can be put back on track somehow in the foreseeable future, a sick society with a bankrupt morality will take much more time to cure. The political and economic institutions of the Soviet civilization are gradually fading away and will soon become merely entries in the history books, but the Soviet mentality, which incorporates a strange mixture of old beliefs with some democratic and free market ideas, will influence life in Russia for a long time; it will carry the birthmark of the totalitarian culture into the twenty-first century.

7

Conclusion

Russia was destined to become a crossroads of political experiments of various kinds throughout history. The first great experiment, which began in October 1917, has now come to an end. Its goal was to build by force a slave socialism and exterminate all who were not fit for that way of life. In Hitler's Germany the idea of "selection" was responsible for eliminating Jews, communists, gypsies, and the insane from their society. In Soviet Russia a huge layer of better-educated, better-skilled, and industrious people were targets for this same elimination.

Now the next experiment is under way, and all that was created during the previous experiment is to be destroyed. A totalitarian socialism is to be converted into a democratic capitalism. Anther grandiose idea.

Apparently, long-suffering Russia seems to be best suited for such experiments—the huge land mass for space and movement, the Babylonian mixture of nationalities and cultures, a patient and resigned people.

The first result of the present experiment—met by some with regret, by others with joy—was the Soviet Union's disappearance from the political map. But many people failed to understand that also destroyed was the whole Soviet civilization—a unique and strange, often ugly and disgusting, sometimes naive and idealistic blend of moral beliefs mingled with economic and political dogmas evident throughout its mass culture, in songs and literature, for seventy years.

However contradictory and hypocritical the Soviet civilization was, its abrupt breakdown has led to the creation of a moral vacuum on one-seventh of the world's land mass—the equivalent of a black hole of permissiveness and violence.

If earlier the rest of the world had feared the spread of communism through Comintern or through the growth of the World Socialist Camp (paid for by "Party gold"), now these countries are threatened by no less a menace than a huge neighbor without a moral center, from which, instead of bolshevism, amorality and crime are beginning to overflow and run into neighboring countries. Fertile soil is being created in Russia for all types of political adventurers—nationalistic, fascist, and criminal.

The earlier threat to the rest of the world posed by the Soviet Union lay in its political and military strength; now paradoxically the menace lies in Russia's weakness, anarchy, and degradation. Obviously, most Western politicians who were trying to weaken the Soviet colossus did not imagine that it might collapse so soon (as if with clay feet), burying its people under the rubble.

Russia is a crippled nation; it is a nation seriously ill. With so many scoundrels and rascal-politicians, the nation cannot get well without understanding this. Russia was dismembered over the course of seven decades, and the organism is struggling to regenerate. Hope is placed in its pieces, the islands of healthy tissue, from which the Russian people might revive.

There has been no radical change, no turning point in public consciousness during this period of collapse and attempted revival; there has been no deep awareness springing from the tenacious horrors of the past. Without repentance, there can be no real negation; the old is growing through the new. The victims are dying, and the butchers have disappeared into the crowd. The people are forgetting the past, without ever having to understand it. Therefore, they are ready for repetition.

If Russia is often called the country with an "unpredictable past," no more predictable is its future. Some trends are beginning to emerge through the turbulent events of the last decade of reforms.

The construction of capitalism or market economy is scarcely being controlled by the changing sets of reformers in government. Privatization of socialist property and the development of private business is influenced more by the conditions of a production crisis and mounting chaos.

In these murky waters of transition from socialism to capitalism, some people will keep trying quick enrichment schemes, and the lack of moral constraints leads many of them to sell or trade fake or tainted food, narcotics, arms, or even human organs. These people continue to use bribes, treat competitors with cruelty, and practically "be in bed" with the criminal world. And the organized criminal groups are with greater frequency controlling business ventures and increasing their influence through law enforcement bodies and state institutions.

Islands of civilized business will emerge slowly in a commercial environment of broken economic ties and destroyed markets, political instability, and controversial and constantly changing economic legislation. All this is making investments risky and unprofitable. Therefore, even the healthy businesses prefer instant deals in trade over more long-range ventures in production and construction.

The majority of the public is frightened by the amoral appearance of young Russian capitalism, and they feel a nostalgia for the old socialism with its low but guaranteed income and its free social benefits—housing, health care, and education. They are searching for a solution in a hybrid of capitalism and socialism embodied in their concepts of the "Swedish model." They would like to acquire the material abundance of capitalism with socialism's social benefits and sense of stability.

As a result, the country grows poorer, and benefits from the state budget keep shrinking, and capitalism is developing qualities shared with the "Wild West."

Some of the younger cohorts, who already grew up under the conditions of the reforms, are taking this semibarbarous environment of immorality and cruelty for granted and accept it as normal. More mature cohorts who curse the dissolution of a stable life style, the savage manners and customs in recent society, and the onslaught of crime and corruption, are gradually getting used to market conditions and the vast possibilities for personal initiative in family farming or small production and service industries. All this is possible with an energetic and entrepreneurial spirit.

Most of the public is either grumbling, or they are silently indignant at the new realities and cannot adapt themselves to capitalism. They don't see any future in it for themselves or for Russia. Certainly, most older cohorts feel that way. And these people dislike those who, in their mind, have brought the country to this circumstance.

For many citizens the real culprits are democracy and the "democrats." One-half of the population regrets that the radical political and economic reform was started in the mid-1980s. And the farther the country moves away from the prereform communist past the more they recall the culture with nostalgia and blame the crisis on today's leaders and reformers, and not on the chiefs of the totalitarian epoch.

Outbursts of enthusiasm and political activity concerning the first innovations of democracy in the late 1980s (free elections and a multiparty system) have been replaced in the mid-1990s with mass political apathy and a dislike of the "democrats," all this when radical economic reform has deepened the crisis and expanded the nation's poverty.

The public is associating democracy with economic chaos and anarchy, and they believe it also leads to the growth of crime. They do not believe that participating in elections or belonging to a political party can better their lot or condition. Therefore, almost half do not take part in elections.

Those who do participate make their choice on the basis of the candidates' appearances on television, using their rhetoric and populist manner, their fierce criticism of those in power, and their impracticable but alluring promises. Because the general political culture of the population is low, the level of political sophistication in their chosen representatives is also quite low.

At one time the aristocrats noted with disdain that in the new democracies the countries are being governed by public opinion, with all its defects—ignorance, emotionality, and contradictions. This interpretation is exactly what is happening in Russia during the early stages of its democracy. The development of a civic society, with its network of numerous public connections (including political parties) that should serve as mediators between people and power, has been slow and suggests to our unpoliticized electorate that they are electing their rulers at random, from whom they soon will turn away in anger. This condition represents an ideal environment in which political demagogues, adventurers, and machinators can flourish, especially those criminal elements which are penetrating politics in increasing numbers.

A fertile soil for the creation of a new Hitler now exists. A growing Russian nationalism and nostalgia for "Greater Russia" are, for the moment, the only substitute for ideology to unite the Russian people, and it may not be enough. As long as these conditions exist, Russia's democratic infancy will be threatened by the possibility of a dictator coming to power with the support of a public seduced by demagoguery and populist slogans, by the newly rich manipulating power, and by organized crime controlling the state agencies.

A power vacuum increases the threat of ethnic conflicts, with neighbors and within Russia, and it also increases the possibility for further separatism and even the dissolution of Russia into independent countries—or into something like a confederacy (or even looser union).

• • •

In the very center of Moscow three subway lines cross. To transfer from one line to another, people have been moving down an escalator for more than 50 years. If you look at the wall above the escalator, you can see under the white plaster a faint relief. If you look more closely, you can make out a human profile. Here in the center of the Moscow subway, a bronze bas-relief of Stalin was once displayed. After the Twentieth Party Congress, it was removed, but no matter how many times this place was plastered and painted over, a trace of the dictator's face is still evident over the heads of millions of passengers, most of whom have no idea about what it means.

Similarly, no matter how much the present-day reformers paint over the traces of the totalitarian civilization in today's society, these images will obtrude into people's consciousness for a long time and make an impact on the course of reforms in areas of the economy, politics, and popular culture.

A decade of these reforms has passed in Russia, and the results are mixed. The empire has dissolved and along with it the totalitarian regime and its ideology. But the economy also disintegrated and with it the fabric of society, stitched together with dictatorship, with its value system, and with its culture.

Medieval Russia with its feudal disunity and internecine clashes became prey to the Mongol-Tartar nomads, and this period resulted in great human losses, slowing down tremendously economic and cultural development. In 1945 the Soviet Union prevailed over Nazi Germany with great sacrifice—millions of people perished and half of the country lay in ruins. The Soviet empire and civilization could not sustain the internal tension and arms race with the West, and it collapsed.

Again Russia is beginning—after huge losses—to build a new society on the ruins of the old. Will it be able to rouse itself and recover? Will the Russian people be able to restore the greatness and national pride of their culture? It has happened in the past. Why can't it happen again?

Appendix
Notes

Appendix

The Russian Center for Public Opinion and Market Research

The Russian Center for Public Opinion and Market Research (Vserossiyskiy Centr Izucheniya Obshchestvennogo Mneniya or VCIOM) was founded in 1988 as the All-Union Center for Public Opinion Research (the acronym in Russian is also VCIOM). Its director was academician Tatyana Zaslavskaya, a well-known economist and sociologist and one of most courageous critics of the totalitarian economic system. Among the cofounders of the center were professors Yuri Levada, director of VCIOM since 1991, and Boris Grushin, who has established his own sociological service, VP, in 1990.

VCIOM was the first organization in the history of Russia and the Soviet Union to conduct national public opinion surveys on a regular basis. It remains today the largest agency engaged in public opinion and market research in Russia and in the other territories of the former Soviet Union. The Center's headquarters in Moscow employ more than 100 full-time researchers and supporting staff. The center operates a network of 32 regional offices, of which 20 are its own branches, which allows it to conduct surveys throughout Russia and on other territories of the ex-USSR. This network uses a common methodology for data gathering throughout, and this provides continuity and comparability of results.

VCIOM is a nongovernmental, commercial organization that provides contractual services for the media, business, government, and academic organizations, Russian and foreign. It conducts regular omnibus surveys of the Russian population and ad hoc specialized studies of public attitudes, in addition to market research studies.

Major omnibus surveys include *monitors* or monthly and quarterly surveys with 88 polling stations and 4000 sample size; *fact,* surveys in 42 sample points and 1650 sample size; and *express,* fast (within a week) surveys of urban population, in 24 sample points with sample sizes of 1600.

• • •

The principle form of data gathering is through the at-home person-to-person interview. It is conducted this way because only one-quarter of all households in Russia have telephones and the telephone system is unreliable. The standard sampling procedure includes three stages. At the first stage the total number of potential respondents is divided into eleven standard economical-geographic regions of Russia, proportionate to their population. These regions are Northern, North-Western, Central, Volgo-Vyatka, Central–Black Earth, Volga Basin, North-Caucasus, Urals, West-Siberian, East-Siberian, and Far-Eastern.

The assigned number of respondents in a region is subdivided among seven strata of population centers:

1. Moscow and St. Petersburg;
2. Oblast, krai administrative centers with a population of more than one million;
3. Oblast, krai centers with less than one million population;
4. Other urban settlements;
5. Administrative centers of national autonomies with population 300,000 and over;
6. Other urban settlements in national autonomies;
7. Rural settlements.

At the second stage the sample points are selected in each region/stratum, proportionate to their weight in the total population.

Respondents are selected by random address or route method at the third stage of sampling. In the address method the residents registration books and voter registration lists are used.

This sampling method provides statistical representation of polling for the total population of Russia. VCIOM conducts about 100 polls yearly. Major findings of these social and economic surveys (*Monitors*) are published in the quarterly, "Economic and Social Change. The Monitoring of Public Opinion," published jointly by VCIOM and The Interdisciplinary Academic Centre for Social Sciences.

Notes

1. Introduction

1. Vladimir Shlappentoch, *Public and Private Life of the Soviet People: Changing Values in Post-Stalin Russia* (New York: Oxford University Press, 1989).

2. Alexander Zinoviev, *Homo Soveticus* (Moscow: Kor-Inf, 1991).

3. Tatyana Zaslavskaya, *The Second Socialist Revolution: An Alternative Soviet Strategy* (London: I. B. Tauris, 1990).

4. Tatyana Zaslavskaya and Rosalina Ryvkina, *Sociology of the Economic Life: Theory Essays* (Novosibirsk: Nauka, 1991).

5. Boris Grushin, *Mass Consciousness: Problems of Definition and Research* (Moscow: Politizdat, 1987).

6. Yuri Levada et al., *There Is an Opinion* (Moscow: Progress, 1990).

2. Perestroika: Socialism with an Honest Face

1. I described this scenario, which was already becoming reality, in a magazine article, "Constitutional Crisis," *New Times* 49 (1990), 4–6. But I could not have predicted the speed with which the inner circle broke apart.

2. Mikhail Gorbachev, *The New Way of Thinking for Our Country and the Whole World* (Moscow: Politizdat, 1987).

3. All Union Center for Public Opinion Research (VCIOM), monthly survey, January 1988.

4. Gorbachev, *New Way,* 32, 33.

3. The New Soviet Man: Myth or Reality?

1. Vladimir I. Lenin, *Works,* 5th ed., vol. 43 (Moscow: Politizdat, 1970), 31.

2. Nicolas Werth, *Histoire De L'Union Sovietique, 1900–1991* (Moscow: Progress-Academia, 1992) 130.

3. Oleg Volkov, *Immersion into the Darkness* (Moscow: Sovetskaya Rossiya, 1992), 5, 6.

4. Nikolai Ostrovsky, *How the Steel Was Tempered* (Moscow: Pravda, 1982).

5. Volkov, 6.

6. Eugenia Ginsburg, *Krutoi marshrut. Khronika vremyen kulta lichnosti.* (Riga: Kursiv, 1989).

4. The Winding Road to Democracy

1. Nikolai Popov, "Public Attitudes Toward Crime and Law Enforcement: A Survey of Public Opinion." Report, 1990.

2. B. A. Grushin, N. P. Popov, A. Finifter, G. Gerbner, E. Mickiewicz, "Television and Society," Soviet-American Study of Public Opinion, report, 1989.

3. Nikolai Popov, "Attitudes Toward Elections," Public Opinion Survey, report, Mar. 1989.

4. VCIOM monthly poll, July 1991.

5. VCIOM monthly survey FACT, May 1993.

6. Popov, "Attitudes," Mar. 1989.

7. VCIOM New Year Poll, Dec. 1990.

8. Nikolai Popov, "Institutions of Power," A Survey of Public Opinion, report, Sept. 1989.

9. Grushin, "Television," Dec. 1989.

10. Popov, "Public Attitudes."

11. VCIOM Survey FACT, Jan. 1992.

12. Ibid., Oct. 1993.

13. Popov, "Attitudes," Mar. 1989.

14. VCIOM Survey FACT, Sept. 1993.

15. Nikolai Popov and Rousina Volkova, "The New Constitution of the Russian Federation and Public Opinion," survey report, Mar. 1991.

16. Popov and Volkova, Mar. 1991.

17. Boris Grushin, "Survey on Democracy," *New Times* 22 (1993): 6.

18. VCIOM Survey FACT, May 1993.

19. Ibid., Feb. 1993.

20. Ibid.

21. Ibid., May 1993.

22. VCIOM Survey Results, *Moscow News*, Dec. 22, 1991.

23. VCIOM Survey FACT, Oct. 1992.

24. Ibid., Feb. 1993.

25. Ibid., Apr. 1993.

26. Ibid., Sept. 1993.

27. VCIOM Survey, Mar. 1993.

28. VCIOM Survey FACT, Oct. 1993.

29. Ibid., Apr. 1993.

30. Ibid., May 1993.

31. Grushin, "Television," Dec. 1989.

32. VCIOM Survey FACT, Oct. 1993.

33. Ibid.

34. Ibid.

35. VCIOM Survey Express, Dec. 5–7, 1993.

36. Ibid., Dec. 17, 1993.

37. Ibid.

5. From Socialism to a Wild West Capitalism

1. VCIOM Survey, Feb. 23, 1993.
2. VCIOM Omnibus Survey, Dec. 1990.
3. Ibid.
4. Ibid.
5. VCIOM Survey FACT, Sept. 1993.
6. Ibid., Oct. 1993.
7. VCIOM Omnibus Survey, Dec. 1990.
8. VCIOM Survey FACT, Aug.–Sept. 1992.
9. VCIOM Quarterly Monitor, July 1993.
10. Nikolai Popov and Sergei Shpilko, "Attitudes about the Law on Property," public opinion survey, report, Dec. 1989.
11. Ibid., Jan. 1990.
12. Ibid.
13. Ibid.
14. Ibid.
15. Ibid.
16. VCIOM Quarterly Monitor, July 1993.
17. Popov and Shpilko.
18. Ibid.
19. Popov and Volkova.
20. Ibid.
21. VCIOM Rural Population Survey, June 1992.
22. Grushin, "Television."
23. Popov and Volkova.
24. Ibid.
25. Ibid.
26. Ibid.
27. VCIOM Quarterly Monitor, July 1993.
28. Nikolai Popov, Vadim Sazonov, and Olga Reznikova, "The Unemployed and Their Problems," survey report, Aug. 1993.
29. VCIOM Survey FACT, June 1993.
30. *Moskovsky Komsomolets,* February 10, 1994.
31. VCIOM Quarterly Monitor, July 1993.
32. "Economic Reform," VCIOM survey, Jan. 1993.
33. Ibid
34. VCIOM Quarterly Monitor, July 1993.

6. Moral Standards at a Time of Change

1. *Moscow News,* no. 23, June 6, 1993.
2. *Moscow News,* no. 9, Feb. 28, 1993.
3. *Moskovsky Komsomolets,* June 25, 1993.
4. Popov, "Public Attitudes."
5. Grushin, "Television."
6. *General Social Surveys, 1972–1988: Cumulative Codebook,* National Opinion Research Center (Chicago: Univ. of Chicago, 1989), 183.

7. H. McClosky and J. H. Schaar, "Psychological Dimensions of Anomie," *American Sociological Review* 30, no. 1 (1965): 14–40.

8. Popov, "Public Attitudes."

9. VCIOM Quarterly Monitor, July 1993.

10. T. W. Adorno, Else Frenkel-Brunswick, D. J. Levinson, and R. N. Sanford, *The Authoritarian Personality* (New York: Harper, 1950).

11. "A Soviet Person," VCIOM Survey, Nov. 1989.

12. *Moskovsky Komsomolets,* Ministry of Internal Affairs Press Briefing, Apr. 17, 1993.

13. Ibid.

14. "Crime and Punishment," no. 4–5, 1993.

15. VCIOM poll, Nov. 1992.

16. Popov, "Public Attitudes."

17. VCIOM Omnibus Survey, Nov. 1991.

18. "Bulletin of Sociological and Budget Surveys," State Committee on Statistics, no. 2, 1991.

19. "Crime and Punishment," no. 4–5, 1993, 10.

20. Ibid., 11.

21. Ibid., 10.

22. VCIOM Survey FACT, Dec. 1990.

23. VCIOM Omnibus Survey, Nov. 1990.

24. Popov, "Public Attitudes."

25. Ibid.

26. *Izvestiya,* Nov. 26, 1991.

27. Popov, "Public Attitudes."

28. Ibid.